At Issue

Is Gun Ownership
a Right?

Other Books in the At Issue Series:

At Issue

Is Gun Ownership a Right?

Lea Sakora, Book Editor

GREENHAVEN PRESS
A part of Gale, Cengage Learning

GALE
CENGAGE Learning™

Detroit • New York • San Francisco • New Haven, Conn • Waterville, Maine • London

Christine Nasso, *Publisher*
Elizabeth Des Chenes, *Managing Editor*

For more information, contact:
Greenhaven Press
27500 Drake Rd.
Farmington Hills, MI 48331-3535
Or you can visit our Internet site at gale.cengage.com

Articles in Greenhaven Press anthologies are often edited for length to meet page requirements. In addition, original titles of these works are changed to clearly present the main thesis and to explicitly indicate the author's opinion. Every effort is made to ensure that Greenhaven Press accurately reflects the original intent of the authors. Every effort has been made to trace the owners of copyrighted material.

Cover image © Images.com/Corbis.

LIBRARY OF CONGRESS CATALOGING-IN-PUBLICATION DATA

Is gun ownership a right? / Lea Sakora, book editor.
    p. cm. -- (At issue)
    Includes bibliographical references and index.
    ISBN 978-0-7377-4428-6 (hardcover)
    ISBN 978-0-7377-4429-3 (pbk.)
    1. United States. Constitution. 2nd Amendment. 2. Firearms--Law and legislation--United States. 3. Gun control--United States. I. Sakora, Lea.
    KF3941.I8 2009
    344.7305'33--dc22

                            2009026389

Printed in the United States of America
1 2 3 4 5 6 7 13 12 11 10 09

Contents

Introduction

In 1997 two young men were on the observation deck of the Empire State Building when a gunman entered the area. He shot both men. One man died; the other man, shot in the head, was critically injured. The gunman then killed himself.

On July 30, 2008, the Illinois Council Against Handgun Violence (ICHV) published a column by the injured young man's brother, Dan Gross. "The shooting changed a lot of our lives forever," Gross said. "I didn't want to change my life to be a flash-in-the-pan based on this tragedy. I wanted my response to be thoughtful as well as emotional. Soon, I realized the magnitude of this issue—and learned that what happened was not unique to my experience."

At the time of the tragedy, Gross was working as a partner in a major advertising company. His focus became the cause of gun violence prevention. He quit his job and—using his background in marketing, media, and communications—created the organization PAX, which emphasizes a public health and safety approach to the gun issue. "We view gun violence as an urgent issue of public safety—an issue that we are all in a position to do something about," Gross said. "What we set out to do is create the changes in attitude and behaviors that can make a difference."

PAX developed campaigns to involve people in ending gun violence. One campaign is called ASK (Asking Saves Kids). PAX wants parents to ask if there is a gun in the house before sending a child over to play. According to the PAX Web site, more than 40 percent of homes with children have a gun, and many of those guns are left unlocked or loaded. Many parents have talked with their children about firearms, but talk is not enough when it comes to natural childhood curiosity. When a child finds a gun in someone's home, there is always the chance the child will play with the weapon. According to the

PAX Web site, tips that make asking the question "Is there a gun where your child plays?" easier include "asking the question along with other things you might normally discuss before sending your child to someone's house—such as seat belts, animals, or allergies." If the answer is yes, parents should ask if the gun is in a gun safe with the ammunition locked away separately.

Another campaign developed by PAX is called SPEAK UP. The PAX Web site describes the campaign as a "national awareness and educational initiative providing students with tools to improve the safety of their schools and communities. Based on the fact that in 81 percent of school shootings the attackers tell other students about their plans beforehand, the SPEAK UP program empowers students to report threats of weapon-related violence." The Web site offers this advice to students who hear about a threat in their school: "Don't ignore it. Don't assume it's a joke. No threat is a joke. Don't try to solve the problem yourself." Threats can be reported to a national hotline—1-866-SPEAK-UP. The hotline was introduced in 2002 and allows students to report weapon-related threats anonymously. More than 30,000 calls have been received by the hotline since its inception.

Making change measurable is a big part of what the organization does, according to Gross in the ICHV article. "We may not solve the whole issue every day, but we are providing people with genuine things they can do to make a difference based on things they care about," he said. "National polling has shown that 19 million parents have asked about guns in the home. The numbers also show that fewer children and teens are dying from guns in this country." Gross believes "that the most successful social awareness movements of our time (such as AIDS, tobacco and drunk driving) all gained critical momentum when they became strongly focused on the public health and safety of the community as a whole and, particularly, our innocent and vulnerable children. PAX is bringing this same insight to the gun violence issue."

In *At Issue: Is Gun Ownership a Right?* authors comment on a variety of topics including the historical, political, legal, and behavioral aspects of gun control.

1

The Right to Own
a Gun Is Guaranteed
by the Constitution

Antonin Scalia and the Reporter of Decisions

Antonin Scalia is an associate justice of the Supreme Court. He received his AB from Georgetown University and the University of Fribourg, Switzerland, and his LLB from Harvard Law School. He was appointed Judge of the United States Court of Appeals for the District of Columbia Circuit in 1982. President Reagan nominated him as an Associate Justice of the Supreme Court, and he took his seat September 26, 1986. The Reporter of Decisions prepares a syllabus of a decision of the Court. The syllabus "constitutes no part of the opinion of the Court but has been prepared by the Report of Decisions for the convenience of the reader."

The Second Amendment was reviewed in the case District of Columbia et al. v. Heller, *which was argued before the U.S. Supreme Court in March 2008. In a 5–4 decision, the Court held that the Second Amendment does protect an individual right to gun ownership and thereby determined that the District of Columbia's ban on handguns was unconstitutional. Justice Scalia wrote the opinion of the Court. The following includes text from the syllabus prepared by the Reporter of Decisions and from Justice Scalia's written opinion.*

Syllabus, and Opinion of the Court, in Supreme Court of the United States, *District of Columbia ET AL. v. Heller*, No. 07-290, 2008, pp. 1–3, 64.

District of Columbia law bans handgun possession by making it a crime to carry an unregistered firearm and prohibiting the registration of handguns; provides separately that no person may carry an unlicensed handgun, but authorizes the police chief to issue 1-year licenses; and requires residents to keep lawfully owned firearms unloaded and disassembled or bound by a trigger lock or similar device. Respondent Heller, a D.C. special policeman, applied to register a handgun he wished to keep at home, but the District refused. He filed this suit seeking, on Second Amendment grounds, to enjoin the city from enforcing the ban on handgun registration, the licensing requirement insofar as it prohibits carrying an unlicensed firearm in the home, and the trigger-lock requirement insofar as it prohibits the use of functional firearms in the home. The District Court dismissed the suit, but the D.C. Circuit reversed, holding that the Second Amendment protects an individual's right to possess firearms and that the city's total ban on handguns, as well as its requirement that firearms in the home be kept nonfunctional even when necessary for self-defense, violated that right.

Assuming he is not disqualified from exercising Second Amendment rights, the District must permit Heller to register his handgun and must issue him a license to carry it in the home.

Held:

1. The Second Amendment protects an individual right to possess a firearm unconnected with service in a militia, and to use that arm for traditionally lawful purposes, such as self-defense within the home. . . .

Individuals Have Second Amendment Rights

2. Like most rights, the Second Amendment right is not unlimited. It is not a right to keep and carry any weapon what-

soever in any manner whatsoever and for whatever purpose: For example, concealed weapons prohibitions have been upheld under the Amendment or state analogues [similar laws]. The Court's opinion should not be taken to cast doubt on longstanding prohibitions on the possession of firearms by felons and the mentally ill, or laws forbidding the carrying of firearms in sensitive places such as schools and government buildings, or laws imposing conditions and qualifications on the commercial sale of arms. *Miller*'s holding that the sorts of weapons protected are those "in common use at the time" [*U.S. v. Miller* (1939)] finds support in the historical tradition of prohibiting the carrying of dangerous and unusual weapons.

The District of Columbia's Handgun Ban Is Unconstitutional

3. The handgun ban and the trigger-lock requirement (as applied to self-defense) violate the Second Amendment. The District's total ban on handgun possession in the home amounts to a prohibition on an entire class of "arms" that Americans overwhelmingly choose for the lawful purpose of self-defense. Under any of the standards of scrutiny the Court has applied to enumerated constitutional rights, this prohibition—in the place where the importance of the lawful defense of self, family, and property is most acute—would fail constitutional muster. Similarly, the requirement that any lawful firearm in the home be disassembled or bound by a trigger lock makes it impossible for citizens to use arms for the core lawful purpose of self-defense and is hence unconstitutional. Because Heller conceded at oral argument that the D.C. licensing law is permissible if it is not enforced arbitrarily and capriciously, the Court assumes that a license will satisfy his prayer for relief and does not address the licensing requirement. Assuming he is not disqualified from exercising Second

Amendment rights, the District must permit Heller to register his handgun and must issue him a license to carry it in the home. . . .

Gun Violence and Gun Rights

We are aware of the problem of handgun violence in this country, and we take seriously the concerns raised by the many *amici* [friends] who believe that prohibition of handgun ownership is a solution. The Constitution leaves the District of Columbia a variety of tools for combating that problem, including some measures regulating handguns. But the enshrinement of constitutional rights necessarily takes certain policy choices off the table. These include the absolute prohibition of handguns held and used for self-defense in the home. Undoubtedly some think that the Second Amendment is outmoded in a society where our standing army is the pride of our Nation, where well-trained police forces provide personal security, and where gun violence is a serious problem. That is perhaps debatable, but what is not debatable is that it is not the role of this Court to pronounce the Second Amendment extinct.

We affirm the judgment of the Court of Appeals.

2

The Right to Own a Gun Is Not Guaranteed by the Constitution

John Paul Stevens

John Paul Stevens is an associate justice of the Supreme Court. He received an AB from the University of Chicago, and a JD from Northwestern University School of Law. From 1970 until 1975, he served as a Judge of the United States Court of Appeals for the Seventh Circuit. President Ford nominated him as an Associate Justice of the Supreme Court, and he took his seat December 19, 1975.

Justice Stevens wrote a forty-six-page dissenting opinion on the District of Columbia v. Heller (2008) case that held that the Second Amendment protects an individual's right to gun ownership. He sees "conflicting pronouncements" with almost every interpretation in the majority opinion, including the amendment's purpose, language, history, nature of a militia, and the role of Congress. Justice Stevens writes that the majority opinion has weaknesses and often lacks accuracy in interpretation.

The question presented by this case is not whether the Second Amendment protects a "collective right" or an "individual right." Surely it protects a right that can be enforced by individuals. But a conclusion that the Second Amendment protects an individual right does not tell us anything about the scope of that right.

John Paul Stevens, "Dissenting Opinion," in Supreme Court of the United States, *District of Columbia ET AL. v. Heller*, No. 07-290, 2008, pp. 1–7, 46.

Guns are used to hunt, for self-defense, to commit crimes, for sporting activities, and to perform military duties. The Second Amendment plainly does not protect the right to use a gun to rob a bank; it is equally clear that it *does* encompass the right to use weapons for certain military purposes. Whether it also protects the right to possess and use guns for nonmilitary purposes like hunting and personal self-defense is the question presented by this case. The text of the Amendment, its history, and our decision in *United States v. Miller*, (1939), provide a clear answer to that question.

The Original Purpose of the Second Amendment

The Second Amendment was adopted to protect the right of the people of each of the several States to maintain a well-regulated militia. It was a response to concerns raised during the ratification of the Constitution that the power of Congress to disarm the state militias and create a national standing army posed an intolerable threat to the sovereignty of the several States. Neither the text of the Amendment nor the arguments advanced by its proponents evidenced the slightest interest in limiting any legislature's authority to regulate private civilian uses of firearms. Specifically, there is no indication that the Framers of the Amendment intended to enshrine the common-law right of self-defense in the Constitution.

The Amendment should not be interpreted as limiting the authority of Congress to regulate the use or possession of firearms for purely civilian purposes.

In 1934, Congress enacted the National Firearms Act, the first major federal firearms law. Sustaining an indictment under the Act, this Court held that, "[i]n the absence of any evidence tending to show that possession or use of a 'shotgun having a barrel of less than eighteen inches in length' at this time has some reasonable relationship to the preservation or efficiency of a well regulated militia, we cannot say that the Second Amendment guarantees the right to keep and bear such an instrument." The view of the Amendment we took in *Miller*—that it protects the right to keep and bear arms for certain military purposes, but that it does not curtail the Legislature's power to regulate the nonmilitary use and ownership of weapons—is both the most natural reading of the Amendment's text and the interpretation most faithful to the history of its adoption.

Specifically, there is no indication that the Framers of the Amendment intended to enshrine the common-law right of self-defense in the Constitution.

Since our decision in *Miller*, hundreds of judges have relied on the view of the Amendment we endorsed there; we ourselves affirmed it in 1980. No new evidence has surfaced since 1980 supporting the view that the Amendment was intended to curtail the power of Congress to regulate civilian use or misuse of weapons. Indeed, a review of the drafting history of the Amendment demonstrates that its Framers *rejected* proposals that would have broadened its coverage to include such uses. . . .

In this dissent I shall first explain why our decision in *Miller* was faithful to the text of the Second Amendment and the purposes revealed in its drafting history. I shall then comment on the postratification history of the Amendment, which makes abundantly clear that the Amendment should not be interpreted as limiting the authority of Congress to regulate the use or possession of firearms for purely civilian purposes.

The Language of the Amendment Is Dissected

The text of the Second Amendment is brief. It provides: "A well regulated Militia, being necessary to the security of a free State, the right of the people to keep and bear Arms, shall not be infringed." . . .

But the right the Court announces was not "enshrined" in the Second Amendment by the Framers; it is the product of today's law-changing decision.

The preamble to the Second Amendment makes three important points. It identifies the preservation of the militia as the Amendment's purpose; it explains that the militia is necessary to the security of a free State; and it recognizes that the militia must be "well regulated." In all three respects it is comparable to provisions in several State Declarations of Rights that were adopted roughly contemporaneously with the Declaration of Independence. Those state provisions highlight the importance members of the founding generation attached to the maintenance of state militias; they also underscore the profound fear shared by many in that era of the dangers posed by standing armies. While the need for state militias has not been a matter of significant public interest for almost two centuries, that fact should not obscure the contemporary concerns that animated the Framers.

The parallels between the Second Amendment and these state declarations, and the Second Amendment's omission of any statement of purpose related to the right to use firearms for hunting or personal self-defense, is especially striking in light of the fact that the Declarations of Rights of Pennsylvania and Vermont *did* expressly protect such civilian uses at the time. . . .

17

Permissible Regulations Will Be Decided in the Future

The Court concludes its opinion by declaring that it is not the proper role of this Court to change the meaning of rights "enshrine[d]" in the Constitution. But the right the Court announces was not "enshrined" in the Second Amendment by the Framers; it is the product of today's law-changing decision. The majority's exegesis [analysis] has utterly failed to establish that as a matter of text or history, "the right of law-abiding, responsible citizens to use arms in defense of hearth and home" is "elevate[d] above all other interests" by the Second Amendment.

Until today, it has been understood that legislatures may regulate the civilian use and misuse of firearms so long as they do not interfere with the preservation of a well-regulated militia. The Court's announcement of a new constitutional right to own and use firearms for private purposes upsets that settled understanding, but leaves for future cases the formidable task of defining the scope of permissible regulations. Today judicial craftsmen have confidently asserted that a policy choice that denies a "law-abiding, responsible citize[n]" the right to keep and use weapons in the home for self-defense is "off the table." Given the presumption that most citizens are law abiding, and the reality that the need to defend oneself may suddenly arise in a host of locations outside the home, I fear that the District's policy choice may well be just the first of an unknown number of dominoes to be knocked off the table. . . .

The Court properly disclaims any interest in evaluating the wisdom of the specific policy choice challenged in this case, but it fails to pay heed to a far more important policy choice—the choice made by the Framers themselves. The Court would have us believe that over 200 years ago, the Framers made a choice to limit the tools available to elected officials wishing to regulate civilian uses of weapons, and to authorize this Court to use the common-law process of case-by-case judicial lawmaking to define the contours of acceptable gun control policy. Absent compelling evidence that is nowhere to be found in the Court's opinion, I could not possibly conclude that the Framers made such a choice.

For these reasons, I respectfully dissent.

3

The Intent of the
Second Amendment Has
Been Misinterpreted

Don B. Kates

Don B. Kates is a research fellow at the Independent Institute, a nonprofit, scholarly research and educational organization, which sponsors comprehensive studies on political economy.

The Second Amendment is widely misunderstood. The Bill of Rights was not a profound statement, but rather a political attempt by anti-federalists to oppose enactment of the Constitution. The Second Amendment ensured a militia, a system that was already part of colonial life and law.

To understand the right to arms (Second Amendment), one must have some background on the whole Bill of Rights. The Bill of Rights is a set of 10 articles amending the original Constitution. It was authored by James Madison and enacted in the First Congress, which followed shortly after the original Constitution was ratified and the new federal government formed.

Over the last half of the 20th century, the Bill of Rights has loomed large in American politics, with the Supreme Court striking down numerous federal, state and local laws as being contrary to some right guaranteed by the Bill of Rights. The trouble is, this modern history has generated a sense of

Don B. Kates, "Understanding the Second: How the Bill of Rights Shaped Today's Gun Rights Debate," *Handguns*, vol. 22, no. 2, April–May 2008, pp. 14, 16. Copyright © 2008 InterMedia Outdoors, Inc. Reproduced by permission.

the Bill of Rights' importance, which tends to obscure how it originated and particularly obscures the meaning of the right to arms.

A Political Ploy

The fact is that the Bill of Rights was just a political ploy, and by the time it passed it was a big yawn to those who passed it. The relevant history is this. After America revolted against Britain in 1775, a number of the new states (former colonies) enacted written constitutions, including lists of rights that laws enacted by those states were forbidden to infringe upon. Most of those lists included the right to arms, which 18th century Americans believed to be part of the first of all rights (as they saw it), the right to self-defense.

In 1787, some of the nation's most prominent statesmen met in Philadelphia to write a constitution for the nation. But some of those men, and other statesmen who had not been there, ended up opposing enactment of the Constitution when it was presented to the states for ratification.

Modern history has generated a sense of the Bill of Rights' importance, which tends to obscure how it originated.

These opponents are now known as the Anti-Federalists. The real issue for them was the many provisions in the Constitution that they did not like. But as a smokescreen they also raised an issue about which they really cared nothing: that the Constitution lacked a bill of rights such as those that many state constitutions had.

Ironically, while the Anti-Federalist objections to various provisions of the Constitution were not persuasive to most Americans, their objection to the lack of a bill of rights struck a chord with the general populace, if not the politicians.

Express Powers

Madison saw no need for a bill of rights. Like the other Federalists, and most of the Anti-Federalists, Madison thought the federal government had only those powers expressly mentioned in the Constitution. If that document did not say the federal government could deal with religion or free speech or guns, then it could not do or legislate anything at all about these subjects.

[Madison's] bill was just a collection of routine late 18th century platitudes—things everyone believed in—including the right to arms.

Naturally, Madison was a leader in the fight to get the states to ratify the Constitution. The bill of rights issue loomed particularly large in his home state of Virginia. It was crucial to have Virginia ratify the Constitution, so Madison promised to introduce into the First Congress a token bill of rights to be adopted as amendments to the Constitution.

Once Virginia and enough other states ratified the original Constitution, the Anti-Federalists had no more interest in the bill of rights issue, but Madison kept his promise, introducing a bill of rights in the First Congress. His bill was just a collection of routine late 18th century platitudes—things everyone believed in—including the right to arms.

The reaction to Madison's proposal was spectacularly lackadaisical. Nobody was opposed to it, but nobody cared because no one seriously thought government would ever violate these universally accepted rights. Madison had difficulty getting his proposal even considered in committee or on the floor.

The Anti-Federalists were no longer concerned with the issue. Nor did Madison's own Federalist party deem it urgent because they agreed with him that the federal government had no power to interfere with freedom of speech, religion, etc. But at Madison's insistence, Congress reluctantly turned its attention to his proposal, which was quickly passed with minor changes.

The importance of this history is that it demolishes both how anti-gunners try to misconstrue the Second Amendment and what many pro-gunners think it means.

Anti-gunners say the amendment overturned the military-militia provisions of the original Constitution. The Anti-Federalists did indeed object to those provisions. But the problem with this is that the amendment's author was not Patrick Henry or any of the other Anti-Federalists. Rather, it was the leading Federalist exponent of the Constitution, Madison, who was not about to weaken or erase federal powers that he himself had written into the [document].

Indeed, Madison repeatedly said his Bill of Rights had not retrenched on federal powers nor changed one word of the original Constitution because its provisions prohibited the federal government only from doing things he believed it had had no power to do in the first place.

Nor were the Anti-Federalists laboring under any delusion that Madison's Bill of Rights retrenched on the federal military-militia powers. They proposed their own amendments aimed at weakening those powers to which they objected. But their proposed amendments were defeated, for the Anti-Federalists were a minority in the First Congress as in the nation generally. As to the Second Amendment, they recognized that it guaranteed individuals a right to arms.

Even as the Anti-Federalists affirmed their agreement with the Federalists—in approving a right to arms—they protested that this did not meet their objections to the original Constitution. But that was something Madison had never promised to do. In fact, his promise was implicitly contrary. He was going to write a Bill of Rights, which meant that document would be under Federalist control.

Requirements of the Militia

But what about the phrase in the Second Amendment that praises the militia? To understand that, one has to understand that "the militia" was a system in which colonial laws required: (1) every respectable man of military age to have a gun and appear with it whenever the militia were called out for training or service; (2) every household had to have a gun even if all its members were exempt from military service; and (3) all men had to carry guns whenever they left their own property. Requirement three was probably not enforced in the seacoast colonies after the danger of Indian attack became remote.

Pro-gunners should not misunderstand the Second Amendment as being primarily about revolting against tyranny. Rather, the amendment was about the right to possess arms for self-defense.

Thus one purpose of the amendment was to preserve the arms of the militia by guaranteeing individually owned arms, which were in fact the arms of the militia.

But pro-gunners should not misunderstand the Second Amendment as being primarily about revolting against tyranny. Rather, the amendment was about the right to possess arms for self-defense, a right that was universally endorsed by our Founding Fathers and the political philosophers they revered, including [Greek philosopher] Aristotle, [English philosopher John] Locke and [French thinker Charles] Montesquieu.

4

The Language of the 1700s Is Key to Understanding the 2nd Amendment

Adam Freedman

Adam Freedman writes the "Legal Lingo" column for New York Law Journal *magazine. Freedman is a lawyer and former editor and columnist for the* Buenos Aires Herald. *He has written widely about Latin America, Europe, and the United States.*

A group of professors of linguistics and English wrote a legal brief to assist the Supreme Court in understanding the literal meaning of the Second Amendment. The Amendment's unusual language is the only sentence of its kind in the entire Constitution. There is no agreement between the linguists and Justice Scalia's interpretation of the Amendment.

On June 26, the U.S. Supreme Court fired off its decision in *District of Columbia v. Heller*, holding by a 5–4 majority that the Second Amendment confers an individual right to possess firearms, unconnected to military service.

Heller—long anticipated as the Court's first-ever comprehensive interpretation of the right "to keep and bear arms"—generated an astounding 67 amicus curiae [adviser to the court] briefs. But of those 67 briefs, the only one cited by both the majority and dissenting opinions was one submitted by a group of professors of linguistics and English, the so-called "Linguists' Brief."

These language mavens took center stage because of the dearth of judicial precedent on the Second Amendment. In the absence of helpful prior decisions, the Court had to start from scratch in decoding the "original meaning" of the amendment. While various briefs cited founding-era dictionaries, only the Linguists devoted their entire brief to the niceties of 18th-century grammar and usage.

No Ordinary Sentence

That may seem like a lot of fuss for a single sentence—but then, this is no ordinary sentence. The Second Amendment says: "A well regulated Militia, being necessary to the security of a free State, the right of the people to keep and bear Arms, shall not be infringed."

You will immediately notice that the sentence has two parts, a "prefatory" [introductory] clause (the bit ending in "State") and an "operative" [what is desired] clause (everything after "State"). The relationship between those two clauses has bedeviled scholars for years. Gun control advocates say the prefatory clause limits the scope of the amendment to militia members, while their opponents claim the operative clause creates an individual right to bear arms that cannot be fettered [restrained] by the preface. Unfortunately, there is nowhere else in the Constitution to look for guidance: the Second Amendment's prefatory clause is the only one of its kind in that document.

In the absence of helpful prior decisions, the Court had to start from scratch in decoding the "original meaning" of the amendment.

The Linguists tell us that the prefatory clause of the Second Amendment is what's known as an "absolute clause," that is, an adverbial phrase that is separate from the main clause of the sentence. Such clauses are called "absolute" because they are grammatically independent from the rest of the sentence—no word in the absolute clause can be said to modify any particular word in the main clause.

On the strength of that grammatical autonomy, some gun enthusiasts argued that the prefatory clause has no impact whatsoever on the operative clause. Professor Nelson Lund of George Mason School of Law, for example, wrote in an academic paper that "the Second Amendment has exactly the same meaning that it would have if the preamble [i.e., prefatory clause] had been omitted." By that logic the amendment might as well read, "A well marbled cut of beef, being necessary for a good roast, the right of the people to keep and bear arms shall not be infringed."

The Linguists attacked Lund's assertion with a [an outburst of numerous] grammar books demonstrating that an absolute clause, while grammatically distinct, "add[s] meaning to the entire sentence." The Linguists' point can be seen in an absolute construction that is still in common use: "Weather permitting, I will go for a walk." In that sentence, "weather permitting" is the absolute clause (tip: such clauses typically involve verbs ending in "-ing"). The main clause stands on its own grammatically, but the absolute clause modifies the speaker's intention to go for a walk.

The majority opinion focuses on the straightforward word "keep" while the dissent spends most of its time on the more ambiguous "bear."

Scalia's Interpretation

The Second Amendment's absolute clause, according to the Linguists, expresses a causal connection; namely ". . . a well regulated militia[, being] necessary to the security of a free [S]tate, the right of the people to keep and bear [A]rms, shall not be infringed." Writing for the majority, Justice Antonin

27

Scalia concedes there is a logical link between the two halves of the sentence, but he argues that the prefatory clause merely announces "a" purpose of the operative clause, not "the" purpose (other purposes of gun ownership include hunting and self-defense). On this reading, the amendment is really about allowing individuals to own guns; the fact that this right happens to bolster the militia is simply a plus.

Scalia reaches this conclusion through a novel interpretive technique: He construes [interprets] the second half of the amendment (the operative clause) before the first half (the prefatory clause). While the dissent criticizes Scalia's method as a rhetorical trick meant to elevate "the right of the people" over "a well regulated [M]ilitia," Scalia insists his re-ordering makes more sense than the original sentence structure. Who knows? Perhaps courts will now favor a back-to-front reading for all of the Constitution's first 10 amendments or, as Justice Scalia might call them, the Rights of Bill.

As the majority spokesman, Scalia had the last word, a fact that may have left the much-cited Linguists feeling as though they had been shooting blanks.

In any event, neither side is entirely happy with the operative clause's right "to keep and bear Arms." The majority opinion focuses on the straightforward word "keep" while the dissent spends most of its time on the more ambiguous "bear."

"Keep" has much the same meaning as it did in 1773, when Samuel Johnson defined it as "[t]o retain; not to lose" and "[t]o have in custody." Standing alone, the right "to keep arms" suggests an individual right to have a gun in your house—preferably locked in a child-proof drawer, but an individual right all the same.

The founders, however, did not create a stand-alone right to "keep arms," they joined it with the right "to bear arms." In the high court, the battle over the Second Amendment's operative clause came down to the question of whether "bear arms" must be understood in an idiomatic or non-idiomatic sense. An idiom is an expression that is peculiar to a language (from Latin idioma, "peculiarity"), and conveys a meaning different from its literal or logical signification.

The Meaning of "Bear Arms"

The dissent argues that in the 18th century, "bear arms" was an idiomatic expression meaning "to perform military service," thus emphasizing the martial purpose of the amendment. Among the many examples quoted in the Linguists' [B]rief is the Declaration of Independence, which denounces King George for forcing American colonists "to bear Arms against their country." The Linguists also cite an academic survey of newspapers, books and pamphlets from the founding era: Of 115 texts using the term "bear arms," all but five did so in a military context.

Faced with the Linguists' evidence, Justice Scalia rather ingeniously contends that in the 18th century the idiomatic sense of "bear arms" only existed when those words were followed by the preposition "against." It's not clear where Scalia got that argument—The Complete Idiom's Guide to the Second Amendment?—but it allows him to conclude that the founders intended "bear arms" in the non-idiomatic sense of "to carry arms."

As the majority spokesman, Scalia had the last word, a fact that may have left the much-cited Linguists feeling as though they had been shooting blanks.

5

Gun Ownership and Use Was Needed to Create, Expand, Maintain America

Alex Massie

Alex Massie is a graduate of Trinity College Dublin and a Scottish journalist. He is a contributor to the Scotsman, *the* Daily Telegraph, *the* New Republic, National Review Online, *and the* Sunday Telegraph.

Foreign observers have a difficult time understanding America's gun culture. Guns have a special place in the history of the United States. Much of American gun culture stems from the frequent use of guns to establish and defend the country.

I am puzzled. Puzzled that is, by the British attitude towards America's gun culture. In the aftermath of the Supreme Court's (in my view) common sense ruling that the 2nd Amendment guarantees an individual, rather than a collective, right to bear arms, British commentators responded by, well, by throwing their hands up in the air and yup wondering at *them there crazy Yanks.* Thus Bryan Appleyard:

> I no longer try to understand the American acceptance of well over 30,000 gun related deaths a year. No other country comes close—though it should be noted that over half are suicides—in other countries people may just kill themselves in different ways so the total gun death figure may be misleading. Either way, the weird complacency remains . . . Gun

Alex Massie, "Why Do Americans Love Guns?" *The Debatable Land*, July 8, 2008. Reproduced by permission of the author.

culture remains one of America's greatest aberrations. It baffles other nations. But there you go.

Thus, too, the BBC's Man in Washington, Justin Webb, who quotes the 2nd Amendment and asks:

> Errr, what does that mean? . . . You can disagree with the majority view, but you cannot escape from it if you live in the United States.

Well, as I say, this befuddlement puzzles me. Like many other foreign commentators, these two (whose views, I would suggest, are representative of the British view of American gun culture) seem to be confusing something that is *exceptional* with something that may be considered *bonkers*. But the former does not imply the latter. And in fact the unique nature (in the Western world) of American gun culture seems, to me at least, firmly rooted in a peculiarly, even uniquely, American set of historical, cultural and legal circumstances. Considered individually, some, or even each of these, might be thought insufficient explanations for America's love affair with the gun; taken collectively they render the matter much less mysterious and, I'd hazard, entirely explicable.

The manner *and* timing *of a country's birth must play some part in defining its culture. The United States was born at the point of a gun and, more to the point, could not have been born* without *it being a gun owning society.*

The Point of a Gun

Other developed countries—Canada, Switzerland—also enjoy high rates of gun ownership, yet do not suffer American levels of gun violence. But, rather importantly, neither Canada nor Switzerland was founded at the point of a gun. Timing matters. I'd suggest that had the United States been in a position to declare independence from Britain in 1676 rather than a century later, American culture might be rather different. As it was, the revolutionaries launched their war just as guns became sufficiently reliable and affordable to be everyday purchases for "ordinary" people. Swiss independence, of course, pre-dates the gun, while Canadian independence was, generally speaking, a peaceful, negotiated affair rather than the consequence of an armed insurrection.

This matters, I think, since the *manner* and *timing* of a country's birth must play some part in defining its culture. The United States was born at the point of a gun and, more to the point, could not have been born *without* it being a gun owning society. In this respect, the fact of an armed society was instrumental to its birth. Is it really any wonder that the folk memory of this obvious truth is as powerful as it has been enduring? Guns—and indeed violence—were, in the American context, an enabler and guarantor of freedom from an unacceptable form of government. (We might argue over the degree of "unacceptability," but the perception of its unacceptability seems more pertinent to this discussion.)

America's "Fighting Men"

Consider too, the importance of where the original (European) Americans had come from. The original American frontier was settled, to a disproportionate extent, by folk from the border counties of northern England, southern Scotland and Ulster. These were not religiously-minded brethren, nor were they the aristocrats of plantation Virginia or the burghers of Massachusetts. They came from, not to put too fine a point on it, hard lands that demanded hard men. Fighting men. They had names such as Nixon, Armstrong, Johnson, Graham, Grant and Carson and, one way or another, for better or for worse, their descendants would make major contributions to American life.

These were, again disproportionately, the people who populated the initial Appalachian frontier, moving south from Pennsylvania to western Virginia and the Carolinas before crossing the mountains into what is now Tennessee and Kentucky. They were the descendants, in many cases, of cattle thieves and brigands [bandits] whom Edinburgh and London had sought to corral and control for a couple of hundred years. Again, a folkish resistance to authority was hard wired into their sense of themselves.

And these were the people who played a major role in expanding the United States beyond its initial boundaries. American independence was won by force and American expansion depended upon it. Sure, the Louisiana Purchase was important, but the great race across the continent relied upon first the gun and then the railroad. The creation of the United States as a continental entity relied upon the use of force; force, of course, that was applied using *guns*. (George Custer's middle name, I'd note in passing, was Armstrong.)

Westward Expansion

Furthermore, the opening of the West (the closing [of] it from an Indian point of view) would become, very quickly, *the* defining element of American iconography. Manifest destiny made real. From the Alamo to Monument Valley, the West was won, and secured, at the point of the gun. Without it, America could not have been built. No wonder, then, that guns became such an integral part of the American story. Remember too, that the mythological element of western expansion was exported to teeming eastern cities even before the frontier finally closed. Equally, the idea of the West played an important part in inculcating, even indoctrinating, recently arrived immigrants into the *idea* of America. This was, in theory at any rate, a self-reliant society in which your best, or at least most constant, friend was your Colt .45. There's a reason for the Western being the greatest, most archetypical, American movie genre of them all. No discussion of America and Americana is sensible without a consideration of John Ford and John Wayne.

The United States endured a civil war fought with gunpowder.

The idea of the west—"Go West, young man!"—remains integral to the idea of America. The cowboy and the homesteader remain the great (and thrilling) icons of contemporary Americana. Route 66 (or what remains of it) and driving across America is still a thrilling voyage of possibility, but it's merely an automated version of the journeys made by those first wagon trails; a trip pregnant with hope and dreams and possibility that somehow, however inchoately [imperfectly], still pays some homage to those original pioneers.

In the West, or at least (and I'd argue this is equally and perhaps even more important) in the Hollywood depiction of the West, the lawman establishes his moral authority at the point of a gun just as the outlaw defies authority through the use of force. (Here too one may witness the playing out of the long-lasting tension between authority and self-reliant individualism that has, I'd argue, been a vital constituent of America's success.)

Remember too that, uniquely amongst countries with high, modern day rates of gun ownership, the United States endured a civil war fought with gunpowder. America was founded under arms and then, nearly a century later, arms would be used to determine, to some extent at least, what *sort* of country the United States would be and, again to some extent, the gun would be used to maintain the very existence of these United States. (Of course, the memory of the Civil War and its attendant humiliations would endure in the South while *reinforcing* a perceived need, psychologically speaking, for an armed citizenry capable of resisting, by force if necessary, the encroachments of central government. Fore-armed is forewarned and you never know when this precaution might prove useful in the future.)

In other words, the creation, expansion and maintenance of the United States relied upon the gun. In those circumstances, is it any surprise that the gun might assume totemic [highly symbolic] significance in American culture? Needless to say, these conditions do not apply in other, older countries.

Guaranteed Gun Ownership

The Constitution matters too. As it happens, I think there are some advantages to not having a written constitution, but if you do have one and you take it as seriously as the Americans do theirs, then it's reasonable to, well, respect it. You might think it regrettable that the Second Amendment guarantees a right to gun ownership (or, as the Supreme Court has ruled, prohibits a blanket ban on gun ownership), but there it is, nonetheless: the Constitution says the state cannot prevent you from owning at least some sort of gun. As I say, this is a sensible interpretation: how, after all, could you have a militia unless the people forming—or potentially forming—the militia in times of crisis were themselves armed? One may think this unfortunate, one may even acknowledge that it helps foster a society in which guns, and their attendant violence, are more widespread, but the fact remains that if you have a written constitution and are determined to honour it in the American fashion, you rather have to honour *all* of it, for better or for worse, in sickness and in health. If that means a more violent society than might otherwise be the case, then so be it.

Personal Reflections

But what, you may say, do I know about guns and America? That's a fair question. My experience of guns runs little further than some (accurate!) rifle shooting at boarding school and the occasional clay pigeon shoot since. I've never owned a gun; nor would I be likely to purchase a handgun even if I still lived in Washington, DC.

On the other hand, in 2004 I did attend America's largest machine gun festival and wrote a mildly overwrought piece about it. Anyway, yes, there was a fellow there dressed in full replica SS [Nazi Secret Service] battle group uniform and, yes, other people asked to be photographed with him. But the great (i.e., 98%) majority of those present seemed to be honest enthusiasts and it was, I freely admit, a fun day out. There's an elemental, visceral thrill to running through the woods firing an Uzi [submachine gun], even if my photographer and I had to operate "undercover" for fear of being unmasked as, and consequently turfed out for being, representatives of the "liberal media." Journalists were not welcome. That, of course, is a reminder of the extent to which the American right feels itself under siege. "There's nothing like this in Scotland is there?" participants asked me, a proposition to which fact, as well as tact, compelled me to agree. It was all very American and, in its way, rather marvellous.

If you were to found a country now, I doubt I would recommend you borrow America['s] gun laws.

Back then, mind you, I lived in one of the most violent cities in America, namely Washington, DC. But the statistics, horrifying enough though they are, are misleading. Most, though obviously not all, gun homicides in DC happen in just a few neighbourhoods. Most, though again obviously not all such crimes, are black men shooting other black men. . . .

But this pathology also seems explicable. Isn't it, perhaps, indicative of the existence of a black underclass that is itself the legacy of segregation with all its consequent exploitation and marginalisation? Perhaps that is too neat, too pat an explanation, but mightn't the alienation felt by many African Americans have something to do with this? I only ask. . . .

Even so, this is not the main or only event. If you were to found a country now, I doubt I would recommend you borrow America['s] gun laws. But starting from where, in an American context one must start, culturally, historically and legally, the status quo seems, to me at any rate, both sensible and, in another sense, inevitable. It is, as they say, what it is. But there are good reasons for why, for better or for worse, it is the way it is. So, yes, consider me puzzled why so many folk find this puzzling. . . .

6

Political Pressure Determines Gun Legislation

Benjamin Wittes

Benjamin Wittes is a fellow and research director in Public Law and Governance Studies for the New Republic.

Politics, not the Second Amendment, determines gun control policies in the United States. There is an assumption that gun rights are a fundamental American right. Citizens fight for gun rights through their legislatures and by ballot proposals.

One thing seemed clear from Tuesday's [March 18, 2008] Supreme Court oral arguments in *District of Columbia v. Heller*. The justices are poised to recognize that the Second Amendment confers on individual Americans the right to own guns. . . . After more than two centuries of judicial negligence and intellectual head-scratching, the Second Amendment seems preponderantly likely to mean something. All of which makes *Heller* a kind of watershed in the making.

Or maybe not.

For something else became clear at oral argument—something that actually has been coming into focus since a lower court tossed out Washington's handgun ban and the briefs began winding their way to the justices: Any right to keep and bear arms that the court recognizes is not going to do all that much. Specifically, it won't preclude the sort of reasonable regulation of firearms ownership that makes up most existing gun control laws.

So what *will* this landmark decision actually change?

Limiting Gun Control

Undeniably, a decision recognizing an individual right to gun ownership will put a limit on how far gun control can go. Those who dream of a gun-free society will have to dream of ratifying a new constitutional amendment; they will no longer be able to ignore that embarrassing provision of the Bill of Rights that they have, for so long, been able to argue does not mean what it so plainly seems to say. A decision recognizing the Second Amendment as an individual right will also force authorities at all layers of government to justify before the courts the benefits of crime control and public safety measures that restrict guns against a countervailing interest. And the courts will have to balance the safety benefits against a recognized right that citizens will, citing a Supreme Court opinion, claim is being impinged [pushed aside].

The Supreme Court has no history of enforcing the Second Amendment.

But a disarmed America was always a fantasy. Policymakers do not make a habit of pushing the constitutional lines in making gun policy. The major restraints holding them back are political, not judicial, and a revived Second Amendment won't change that.

The Second Amendment Lacks Judicial Enforcement

Americans have this notion of the courts as the guarantors of the Bill of Rights. But in the case of gun rights, this has never been true. The Supreme Court has no history of enforcing the Second Amendment. Despite the prevalence of guns in American society, a vibrant gun trade, a lot of gun crime, and routine prosecutions of those crimes over decades, the court has developed nothing remotely resembling a developed Second Amendment jurisprudence [philosophy of law]. We still argue about the text and history of the amendment because, with the exception of a cryptic 1939 opinion, there's essentially no case law interpreting it.

Once the people internalize a right as fundamental, it's hard to take it away, even if the courts ignore the issue.

Yet gun rights have not shriveled. To the contrary, they have fared remarkably well in the absence of judicial enforcement. Outside of Washington, D.C., Americans are allowed to own handguns; in many places, the law permits them to carry [handguns] concealed. Yes, restrictions exist. But the impact of 200 years of judicial negligence has not been the atrophying of the right to own weapons. For most noncriminal Americans, packing heat remains an option, albeit one subject to modest government regulation. In fact, if the Supreme Court goes the route implied by this week's [March 2008] oral argument, the justices would largely be codifying and ratifying what is already a national norm that they had little to do with shaping.

Political Pressure Makes Gun Rights Untouchable

Gun rights have remained a part of our national consciousness—and operative law—because of political pressure from an engaged constituency willing to fight for them legislatively and at the ballot box. The strength of the gun lobby made Second Amendment rights untouchable politically even when the judicial climate seemed most tolerant of gun control. The lesson is that once the people internalize a right as fundamental, it's hard to take it away, even if the courts ignore the issue. . . .

But the irony of the gun owners' success is that any new judicial solicitude [concern] for the Second Amendment has

ucted language: "A well regulated Militia, being neces-
o the security of a free State, the right of the people to
and bear arms, shall not be infringed."

ndgun Ban to End

immediate result of the ruling in *District of Columbia v.
ler* was to strike down Washington's tough 32-year-old ban
handguns and its trigger-lock requirement on other fire-
ms, which the city had said were essential to contain vio-
nce in the nation's capital.

The original plaintiff, Washington resident Dick Heller,
aid immediately after the decision was handed down that he
would seek a handgun permit soon, but it may be weeks or
months before the Washington bureaucracy, unaccustomed to
handling gun permits, is ready to act. Mayor Adrian Fenty expressed disappointment at a press conference, adding, "More
handguns will lead to more handgun violence."

---

*[Justice] Scalia wrote that the right he was announcing,
as with other constitutional rights, "is not unlimited."*

"This is a great moment in American history," Wayne LaPierre, vice president of the National Rifle Association [NRA],
said in a statement. The NRA did not initiate the Washington
challenge but eventually embraced it. But Chicago Mayor Richard Daley, whose city has a handgun law similar to
Washington's, said the decision could bring a "return to the
days of the Wild West," according to news reports.

The high court ruling was the last opinion issued by the
justices before adjourning for the summer, striking a discor-
dant note at the end of an otherwise fairly harmonious term.
The court issued far fewer 5–4 decisions this term than it had
handed down the previous term.

limited capacity to give them more than they have already
taken for themselves through the democratic process. For all
but the hardest-core gun lovers, prudence and public safety
ultimately limit libertarianism [a philosophy of limited gov-
ernment]—and the justices don't seem inclined to dive off a
cliff and read the amendment so as to permit individual ownership of upper-end military hardware. That seemed almost as
clear at arguments as the court's direction on the question of
whether the Second Amendment protects an individual right.
A lawyer for those challenging the ban acknowledged, for example, that "of course" background checks for firearms purchases would be constitutional. Justice Antonin Scalia told So-
licitor General Paul Clement, "I don't see why" the federal
government would "have a problem" sustaining its ban on
machine guns if D.C.'s handgun ban fell. All sides appeared
comfortable with the idea that criminals would not receive
protection from the amendment. Outside of Washington, D.C.,
in other words, a revitalized Second Amendment would largely
forbid what nobody was seriously contemplating anyway: bans
on common weapons for the recreational and self-protective
uses of law abiding people.

But inside of Washington—*my hometown* and a city with
a strong local consensus in favor of its handgun ban—*Heller*'s
impact could be big. It remains to be seen whether the Supreme Court will immediately doom the D.C. law or whether
it will, as Clement *has urged*, touch off a new round of litigation over whether the ban constitutes a reasonable regulation
of whatever individual right the justices recognize. Sooner or
later, however, the D.C. handgun ban seems likely to fall. And
if and when that happens, it will be a big change of policy for
the city—and an unpopular one.

I suspect the change won't be hugely consequential in
practical terms. Crime will neither spike (as gun control advocates fear) nor plummet (as the gun rights crowd hopes) as a
result. Washington's streets are already awash in firearms, and

it's hard to believe the introduction of a comparatively small number of highly regulated weapons among those residents without criminal records will measurably impact the number of murders in either direction.

The big change, rather, is a spiritual one. Washington has been the American jurisdiction most willing to dream of a gun-free society. For Washington, a Second Amendment that means something would end an existing experiment. It would impose a national norm on a dissenting local political culture. I'd be more sentimental about the end of that experiment if its results over three decades had been more encouraging. Still, whenever a right goes from a norm to a matter of actionable law—something the courts make sure "shall not be infringed"—it does so at some cost to popular sovereignty, a cost that Washington residents seem fated in this instance to bear.

The Supreme Court Supports an Individual's Right to Bear Arms

Tony Mauro

Tony Mauro is Supreme Court correspondent for American Lawyer Media and Law.com.

The Supreme Court declared for the first time that [the Second] Amendment protects an individual right—not a collec[tive or mi]litia right—to keep and bear firearms for self-defense. [The rul]ing impacts many levels of government. The District of [Colum]bia will need to set aside its handgun ban and develop pr[ocedures] to issue gun permits. Governments throughout the count[ry will] review their current gun control restrictions to determine [if they] conflict with the new Supreme Court ruling. The Court di[d not] "define a standard of review for judging which restrictions a[re or] are not constitutional, and it did not specifically rule that [the] Second Amendment applies to the states." Therefore, many ne[w] lawsuits are expected to help clarify the limits of gun control.

In a historic 5–4 decision Thursday [June 26, 2008], the U.S. Supreme Court declared for the first time that the Second Amendment protects an individual right—not a collective or militia right—to keep and bear firearms for self-defense.

The ruling ended the court's nearly 70-year aversion to considering the meaning of the Second Amendment's oddly

Tony Mauro, "Amendment High Court: 2nd Amendment Protects Individual Right," *The Legal Intelligencer*, June 27, 2008. Copyright © 2008 ALM Media, Inc. Reproduced by permission.

The Right to Bear Arms Extends to Individuals

In the gun case, Justice Antonin Scalia led the majority in analyzing the words of the Second Amendment and the views of its framers and concluding that "they guarantee the individual right to possess and carry weapons in case of confrontation."

But the landmark ruling, which placed bitter divisions of the court on full display, is likely to mark the beginning, not the end, of litigation over Second Amendment rights as gun owners and local governments test the contours of the right enunciated by the court.

Scalia wrote that the right he was announcing, as with other constitutional rights, "is not unlimited." The ruling should not "cast doubt," he added, on restrictions such as barring possession of firearms by felons or the mentally ill or forbidding carrying arms near schools or in government buildings. He also indicated that the use of certain types of weapons could be restricted without running afoul of the Second Amendment.

> "Since this case represents this court's first in-depth examination of the Second Amendment, one should not expect it to clarify the entire field."

But the majority did not define a standard of review for judging which restrictions are or are not constitutional, and it did not specifically rule that the Second Amendment applies to the states—a step that the court has taken in the past to ensure that other parts of the Bill of Rights limit state as well as federal restrictions on individuals.

Both omissions from the ruling virtually guarantee a wave, if not a generation, of legal battles.

Scalia suggested as much in his 64-page opinion when he wrote, almost defensively, "Since this case represents this court's first in-depth examination of the Second Amendment, one should not expect it to clarify the entire field."

The Scope of Gun Rights Is Still Undetermined

In dissent, Justice John Paul Stevens also said the majority's bottom line "does not tell us anything about the scope of that right."

Stevens clashed with Scalia over the meaning of *United States v. Miller*, the 1939 decision that briefly discussed the Second Amendment. To Stevens, that decision defined the Second Amendment as pertaining to militia gun use. But it meant the opposite to Scalia, who was joined by Chief Justice John Roberts Jr. and Justices Anthony Kennedy, Clarence Thomas and Samuel Alito Jr.

Stevens' unusually pointed dissent accused the majority of injecting the court into what are essentially political debates over gun control. The decision, he wrote, "will surely give rise to a far more active judicial role in making vitally important national policy decisions than was envisioned at any time in the 18th, 19th, or 20th centuries."

By contrast Scalia insisted that he was acting with judicial modesty.

"Undoubtedly some think that the Second Amendment is outmoded in a society where our standing army is the pride of our Nation, where well-trained police forces provide personal security, and where gun violence is a serious problem," Scalia wrote. "That is perhaps debatable, but what is not debatable is that it is not the role of this Court to pronounce the Second Amendment extinct."

Justice Stephen Breyer also penned a dissent, arguing that even if the Second Amendment articulates an individual right, the Washington gun ban is reasonable and constitutional. As a response to high levels of urban violence, Breyer said, the handgun ban is "a permissible legislative response to a serious, indeed life-threatening, problem."

Justices David Souter and Ruth Bader Ginsburg joined both dissents but did not write separately.

Gun control supporters, while disappointed with the ruling, said it could have been worse.

The ruling represented a victory for Scalia not only in its result but also in the methodology justices used in their opinions, said Northwestern University School of Law professor John McGinnis. "All justices adopted an originalist approach, suggesting that originalism commands consensus support, at least when the issue is whether a right that is in the Constitution can be restricted."

Cato Institute scholar Robert Levy, who was the financial backer of the challenge to the Washington gun law, said Thursday the court had finally rediscovered the Second Amendment. "Because of Thursday's decision, the prospects for reviving the original meaning of the Second Amendment are now substantially brighter."

The NRA's LaPierre said, "I consider this the opening salvo [saving clause] in a step-by-step process of providing relief for law-abiding Americans everywhere [who] have been deprived of this freedom."

Gun control supporters, while disappointed with the ruling, said it could have been worse.

"Our fight to enact sensible gun laws will be undiminished," said Paul Helmke, president of the Brady Campaign to Prevent Gun Violence in a statement. "While we disagree with the Supreme Court's ruling, which strips the citizens of the District of Columbia of a law they strongly support, the decision clearly suggests that other gun laws are entirely consistent with the Constitution."

8

The Supreme Court's Support of Individual Gun Ownership Is Too Limited

Radley Balko

Radley Balko is a senior editor at Reason *magazine and Reason.com. Previously, Balko was a policy analyst for the Cato Institute, where his specialty was civil liberties issues.*

The District of Columbia v. Heller *Supreme Court ruling determined that individuals have a right to keep and bear arms with broad exceptions. This right is only for self-defense in one's home. Other types of restrictive gun laws are not affected by the ruling. The narrow presentation of the case (the rights of one individual) before the Court helped ensure that the Supreme Court could offer a limited judicial opinion that can only be considered a symbolic victory for individual rights at best.*

For all of the hype, last week's [June 26, 2008] Second Amendment ruling by the Supreme Court won't have much practical effect, at least in the short term. And we likely won't know its long-term implications for years.

D.C. v. Heller wasn't so much a victory for gun rights as it was a deft aversion [skillful turning away] of defeat. The Supreme Court addressed its first broad gun rights case in decades and came away finding that the Constitution confers an individual right to bear arms, not a collective right. A 5–4 decision the other way would have been devastating.

Radley Balko, "A Hollow Victory? Assessing the Real World Impact of *D.C. v. Heller*," *Reason.com*, July 2, 2008. Reproduced by permission.

A Hollow Victory

Still, this victory seems hollow. Perhaps that's in part because of the narrow way the case was argued by the plaintiff, D.C. security guard Dick Anthony Heller.

[Justice] Scalia seems to have gone out of his way to explain that the Court wasn't invalidating laws against concealed carry, laws against "unusual or dangerous" weapons, licensure and permit laws, or laws against possessing weapons in "sensitive areas."

Heller's lawyers' strategy (a wise one, in my opinion) was to argue the case narrowly enough that courts couldn't throw it out, forcing the federal court system once and for all to determine whether the Second Amendment's right to keep and bear arms applies strictly to militias or to each of us as individuals.

Writing for the majority, Justice Antonin Scalia ruled for the latter, but with some broad exceptions.

And there's the rub. Scalia's opinion says the Second Amendment's "individual right" to bear arms extends only to self-defense and, even then, only in one's home. Perhaps in part to help secure a five-vote majority, Scalia seems to have gone out of his way to explain that the Court wasn't invalidating laws against concealed carry, laws against "unusual or dangerous" weapons, licensure and permit laws, or laws against possessing weapons in "sensitive areas."

Second Amendment scholar Nelson Lund writes that Scalia's exceptions could be significant: Should white-collar felons guilty of nonviolent crimes such as tax evasion or insider trading be barred forever from possessing a gun for self-defense?

Scalia's "sensitive areas" might well include the likes of post-Katrina New Orleans—places where the government is striving to preserve order but where the citizens are in most need of arms for self-defense.

Most significantly, [the] decision neglected to incorporate the individual right to gun ownership to the states through the Fourteenth Amendment.

Scalia's opinion also neglected to embrace the Second Amendment as a bulwark against government tyranny, an argument that may at first blush seem anachronistic [out of place] and impractical but that history shows ought not be taken lightly.

One needn't be a modern-day mountain militiaman to observe that authoritarian regimes often become tyrannical after first disarming the citizenry. As Thomas Jefferson put it, "When the people fear their government, there is tyranny; when the government fears the people, there is liberty."

Rights of Individuals Not Extended to States

Most significantly, Scalia's decision neglected to incorporate the individual right to gun ownership to the states through the Fourteenth Amendment. That means that for practical purposes, the only people directly affected by the ruling are the 600,000 residents of Washington, D.C., and the handful of others living in protectorates of the federal government.

To be fair, the plaintiff in the case was a resident of Washington, D.C., and didn't ask the Court to address incorporation. Still, Scalia broached [brought up] the matter in a footnote but was vague and ambivalent about his intentions, leading to competing interpretations over whether he would or wouldn't be amenable [responsive] to incorporation.

Scalia has tended to be skeptical of the idea of broadly applying the Bill of Rights to the states. He also has a history of prioritizing his law-and-order instincts over his allegiance to limited government principles and originalism. . . .

Until the incorporation issue is resolved—which likely will take years—last week's decision, while symbolically significant, has limited practical effect. It means only that the citizens of Washington, D.C., and other federal protectorates have the right to own a handgun for the purpose of self-protection.

But that right only extends to gun ownership in the home, and even then, it's subject to all sorts of restrictions and licensure requirements. Just how strict those requirements can be (could D.C. pass a six-month waiting period for handgun purchases?) will need to be resolved by litigation.

Outside of D.C., nothing has changed. The *Heller* decision won't affect other cities with gun restrictions as severe as those in D.C. So-called "assault weapon bans" [are still] valid. All *Heller* did outside the nation's capital was remove the possibility that Congress might one day pass a blanket federal ban on all firearm ownership, which seemed like a remote possibility, anyway.

[Step] back a bit and the cause for skepticism grows. The Bill of Rights never was intended to be a list of the only rights we have; in fact, the founders worried that future generations might interpret it that way, which is why they included the Ninth and Tenth amendments.

Rather, the Bill of Rights includes the rights the founders considered most important, those necessary to secure and preserve all of the others.

The right to bear arms appears second on the list. And yet even here, on an issue that's become a central tenet of conservative philosophy, we have a decision written by the Court's most conservative justice that can't even uphold the second addition to the Bill of Rights without a series of caveats, exceptions, and asides. And it's a ruling that, practically speaking, applies that right to only a sliver of the country's 300 million residents.

A Long Road to Restore Individual Liberty

As the short-lived "federalism revolution" demonstrates, an incrementalist [bit by bit] approach to winning back the liberties we've lost over the years isn't likely to be successful. Indeed, the general trajectory [path] of the Court over American history has—with some exceptions—been toward more power for the government at the expense of individual liberty, not the other way around.

Heller was a symbolic victory, and the lawyers who brought the longshot case should be commended. But time will tell if this symbolic victory evolves into a practical one.

For now, we're still a long way from a blanket, real-world right to keep and bear arms.

9

The Supreme Court Supports the Development of Common Sense Gun Laws

The Brady Center to Prevent Gun Violence

The Brady Center to Prevent Gun Violence is a national non-profit organization working to reduce the tragic toll of gun violence in America, through education, research, and legal advocacy. The programs of the Brady Center complement the legislative and grassroots mobilization of its sister organization, the Brady Campaign to Prevent Gun Violence.

The Supreme Court's decision in the 2008 case District of Columbia et al. v. Heller *may lead to the passage of more reasonable gun laws in the future. The foundation for this shift is the finding that individuals have a right to gun ownership but that right is lawfully curtailed by a number of broad exceptions. The ruling dismisses the "slippery slope" argument that any gun control would lead to a general ban on guns. The court decision places no restrictions on state or local gun laws.*

The Supreme Court's 5–4 decision in *District of Columbia v. Heller* declared a private right to arms, dramatically changing the long-settled meaning of the Second Amendment; struck down the District of Columbia's ban on handguns as unlawful; and inspired lawsuits against similar bans in other cities. The *Heller* decision, and its questionable reasoning, creates risks to gun laws that criminal defendants and the gun lobby will likely attempt to exploit. Nonetheless, the long-term effects of the decision are at odds with the day-after headlines proclaiming a seminal victory for "gun rights."

The Court went out of its way to make clear that most gun laws are "presumptively" [accepted as true] constitutional while also putting to rest gun owners' fears of a total ban or ultimate confiscation of all firearms. By taking the extremes of the gun policy debate off the table, *Heller* has the potential to allow genuine progress in implementing reasonable gun restrictions, while protecting basic rights to possess firearms. The unintended consequence of *Heller* is that it may end up "de-wedgeifying" one the of the more divisive "wedge" issues on the political landscape: guns. The net result of *Heller* would then be positive by leading to the enactment of the strong gun laws that we need—and the vast majority of Americans want—to protect our communities from gun violence.

Decision's Effect Is Limited

A narrow 5–4 majority of the Supreme Court in *Heller* held that the Constitution provides private citizens with a right to arms, rejecting the view—held by virtually every previous court in our nation's history—that the Second Amendment's militia clause and history limit the right of arms to service in a "well-regulated militia." But the practical effect of the decision is likely to help, not hurt, the cause of preventing gun violence in America.

The direct effect of *Heller* is that the District of Columbia's ban on handguns was invalidated. As Justice [Antonin] Scalia put it in the Court's opinion, the Second Amendment protects "the right of law-abiding, responsible citizens to use arms in defense of hearth and home." However, other than the Washington, D.C., law struck down by the Court, only Chicago and a handful of suburban Chicago jurisdictions have a handgun ban. And even those bans may not be struck down under *Heller*. Because the District is a federal enclave, whether the Second Amendment is "incorporated" against the states was "a question not presented by this case," and the Court cited its earlier decisions that "reaffirmed that the Second Amendment applies only to the Federal Government." Therefore, unless and until the Court holds otherwise, the Second Amendment does not restrict state or local laws. As direct precedent, *Heller* could not be used to support the invalidation of any other gun law in America.

It is also likely that the gun lobby will seek to have courts invalidate sensible gun laws that protect our families from gun violence.

Not only are the gun bans impacted by *Heller* few and far between, but they are the only gun violence prevention proposals that do not consistently garner overwhelming public support. Compare [the] Pew Research Center for the People & the Press, April 23–27, 2008, finding that 59% of Americans oppose a handgun ban with [the] Greenberg Quinlan Rossner & The Tarrance Report poll finding that 67% of Americans favor an assault weapon ban. Taking such bans off the table of policy options will have little effect on the national debate over what effective, politically viable gun violence prevention proposals should be enacted.

A New Legal Weapon

There are, of course, other potential unintended consequences of *Heller* that are not at all positive. There are important potential legal risks presented by the Court's recognition of a private right to arms unrestricted to militia use. Criminal defendants (and their defense lawyers) can be expected to try to transform *Heller* into a "get out of jail free" card, to attempt to evade punishment for serious gun crimes. Some have already begun to argue that the unlawful possession or use of a gun was an "exercise of their Constitutional right to keep and bear arms." While those attacks have been unsuccessful so far, it is possible that prosecutors will be more likely to agree to a plea bargain, or that a different judge, facing different facts, could allow a criminal to walk free based on a misguided extension of the *Heller* ruling.

It is also likely that the gun lobby will seek to have courts invalidate sensible gun laws that protect our families from gun violence, and to prevent the implementation of future laws, using an expanded—and, we believe, unfounded—interpretation of *Heller*. Justice [Stephen] Breyer warned of potential "unfortunate consequences" of the decision:

> The decision will encourage legal challenges to gun regulation throughout the Nation. Because it says little about the standards used to evaluate regulatory decisions, it will leave the Nation without clear standards for resolving those challenges. And litigation over the course of many years, or the mere specter of such litigation, threatens to leave cities without effective protection against gun violence and accidents during that time.

In addition to lawsuits filed since *Heller* [that attack] the handful of other handgun bans—in the Chicago area and San Francisco's housing authority—the gun lobby pushed for a federal bill to invalidate most of Washington, D.C.'s gun laws, using the *Heller* decision as a pretext. Although the bill would strike down regulations of the sort that Justice Scalia noted were "presumptively lawful," and even would have allowed the open carrying of assault weapons on the streets of Washington, the bill was titled "to restore Second Amendment rights in the District of Columbia." The bill exposed the gun lobby's desire to use the narrow holding of *Heller* as a "Trojan Horse [a trap or trick]," arguing that the Second Amendment demands "any gun, any where" policies that the Court pointedly rejected.

While there is little question that *Heller* will inspire an onslaught of legal challenges to our nation's gun laws, and spurious arguments for dangerous gun policies, we believe that the decision, properly read, should not restrict the ability of communities to enact strong laws to keep deadly weapons off our streets and out of the hands of dangerous persons. . . .

The Justices unanimously agreed that virtually all existing gun laws are constitutional, regardless of the Second Amendment's meaning.

Current Gun Laws Are Supported

The Second Amendment, as interpreted by the *Heller* Court, should not pose an impediment to strong reasonable gun laws. The policy proposals favored by the Brady Campaign, and most Americans, are not among those policy options taken off the table by *Heller*. Rather, they are narrowly tailored to minimize gun violence and prevent criminal use of guns, while allowing for possession of conventional handguns and long guns for lawful purposes. For example, we support:

- Universal criminal background checks for all gun sales that eliminate the loophole under which criminals can now buy guns from "private sellers" without a background check at gun shows and elsewhere, no questions asked;

- One-handgun-a-month laws that prevent high volume handgun purchases by gun traffickers;

- Repeal of various restrictions on federal enforcement power against corrupt gun dealers;

- Restrictions on military-style assault weapons (with exceptions for law enforcement and the military), while not preventing lawful purchases of conventional handguns, rifles, and shotguns.

These reasonable proposals should be permitted under *Heller*. While the Justices were narrowly split over whether the Second Amendment was limited to a militia-based right, the Justices unanimously agreed that virtually all existing gun laws are constitutional, regardless of the Second Amendment's meaning. . . .

Shaky Legal Reasoning

Despite the potentially positive effects of *Heller*, its shaky legal reasoning should not be ignored. Especially when the gun lobby and criminals attempt to extend the opinion far beyond its language, courts must be reminded that the right discovered by five Justices in *Heller* was not supported by the Second Amendment's text or history. Many legal scholars still firmly believe that the decision by Justice Scalia and four fellow Justices that the Second Amendment protects a right to bear arms unrelated to participation in a state militia was incorrect. Virtually every court in American history that had construed the Amendment had been swayed by the historical record that makes the militia-centric purpose of James Madison and the other Framers undeniable, as well as by the inconvenient fact that the Amendment begins by expressly referencing its one purpose—"a well-regulated militia, being necessary to the security of a free State." The last time the Court considered the Amendment's meaning, in *U.S. v. Miller* (1939), it unanimously stated that [the Amendment] "must be interpreted and applied" in accord with its "obvious purpose to assure the continuation and render possible the effectiveness" of a well-regulated militia. Nonetheless, Justice Scalia somehow found that the Amendment served purposes unstated in its text, stating "[t]he prefatory clause does not suggest that preserving the militia was the only reason Americans valued the ancient right." Unencumbered by history, the *Miller* precedent, or the militia-centric language chosen by the Framers, Scalia read the Second Amendment as if its first 13 words didn't exist. So much for "judicial restraint," "original intent," and "respect for precedent." . . .

The Law of Unintended Consequences

As students of the Constitution and American history, we believe that Justice [John Paul] Stevens' opinion, also representing the views of Justices Breyer, [David] Souter, and [Ruth Bader] Ginsburg, better reflects the meaning of the Second Amendment and the intent of its Framers than the majority opinion of Justice Scalia. However, in the real world, the *Heller* decision will likely mark a historic example of another law—the law of unintended consequences. By making clear that the Constitution does not permit broad gun bans such as the District's, while allowing for strong reasonable gun laws, the *Heller* decision could well mark a turning point that leads to our nation finally addressing our gun violence problem in a sane and sensible way.

10

School Gun-Free Zone Restrictions Have No Effect on Criminals

Benedict D. LaRosa

Benedict D. LaRosa is a historian and writer with undergraduate and graduate degrees in history from the U.S. Air Force Academy and Duke University, respectively.

Gun control laws are useless in preventing gun violence on campus. Law-abiding students, employees, and visitors are prohibited from carrying concealed weapons on the campus of Virginia Tech University. But in 2007 a lone gunman legally obtained a gun, killed thirty-three students and faculty, and wounded ten others.

Last year [in 2006], Virginia Tech University successfully lobbied the state legislature to prohibit concealed-permit holders from carrying a sidearm on campus. At the time, university spokesman Larry Hincker commented,

> I'm sure the university community is appreciative of the General Assembly's actions because this will help parents, students, faculty, and visitors feel safe on our campus.

In June of last year [2006], the university reemphasized its ban on carrying guns on campus by students, employees, and visitors. . . . It disciplined a student with a concealed-carry permit who brought his handgun to class. On April 16, 2007,

Benedict D. LaRosa, "Gun Control Claims More Victims," *Freedom Daily*, November 2007. Copyright © 2007 The Future of Freedom Foundation. All rights reserved. Reproduced by permission.

43 students and faculty members paid the price for such short-sightedness when a deranged student killed 33 and wounded the remainder with handguns.

Despite claims to the contrary, this is not the worst school killing in U.S. history. On May 18, 1927, a disgruntled school-board member killed 45 people and injured 58—most of them second-grade to sixth-grade children—when he set off bombs at Bath Consolidated School in Bath, Michigan.

To a criminal or deranged person bent on killing, a gun-free zone is a free-fire zone.

In response to the Virginia Tech incident, gun-control advocates predictably demanded more gun-control laws. Carolyn McCarthy (D-N.Y.), author of the latest assault-weapon ban making its way through Congress, which is a more draconian [severe] version of the Clinton 1994 assault-gun ban that expired in 2004, suggested that we need to talk about guns on campus. For once, I agree with Representative McCarthy.

Gun-Free Zones Are the Problem

The gunman, Cho Seung-Hui, a Korean national with permanent resident status, had filled out the required forms and undergone the mandatory background check and waiting period, proving once again the uselessness of such laws.

The problem at Virginia Tech was not that there were guns on campus—only the campus police and gunman were armed—but that it was a "gun-free zone." As a result, there were not enough people carrying guns to neutralize the gunman once he began his rampage. He should have been out-gunned after his first shots. To a criminal or deranged person bent on killing, a gun-free zone is a free-fire zone. As is obvious from all such incidents, the police arrive too late to prevent multiple killings.

61

That's not to disparage [belittle] the police. In most cases, they act aggressively and competently. But they are rarely the first to arrive at the scene of a crime. The first ones there are the perpetrators and their victims. That's when self-defense weapons are needed, not after the damage is done.

Consider that in all such incidents, the shooters are not so deranged as to attack police stations, shooting ranges, or gun shows. They have enough presence of mind to assail unarmed people in gun-free zones because they will encounter no effective resistance. (The one incident in which an individual was foolish enough to threaten to kill hostages where guns were prevalent was at a shooting club in California in July 1999. The gunman was promptly shot by an employee, without harm to the hostages.)

Test my hypothesis. Was anyone carrying a gun killed or injured in the Virginia Tech shooting? Only one, the perpetrator by his own hand. All the other victims were unarmed. They were unarmed because of state law, university policy, the success of gun-control advocates, and a false sense of security. The gun-control lobby has succeeded in stigmatizing gun possession and training; influencing legislators to pass laws making it difficult for law-abiding people to purchase, carry, and use firearms; and convincing people that they can depend on the police to protect them. The students are also at fault for believing the lie that they are not responsible for their own protection in the face of common sense and history.

Handguns and Self-Defense

Handguns are self-defense tools. They are designed to protect people from those who would harm them. In many cases, merely the appearance of a firearm dissuades an attacker. When you prevent people from carrying self-defense weapons, you are making them easy targets.

Let's look at some examples to illustrate my point:

In 1974, 34 Israeli students were gunned down in a bus on a school trip. Israel responded by arming teachers, administrators, bus drivers, and others to protect their children. Israel has not had a repeat of that tragedy. The U.S. government's response? Prohibit guns within 1,000 feet of schools, as if criminals and deranged people obey laws.

In October 1997, Assistant Principal Joel Myrick used a gun to stop a violent teen who was shooting up his high school in Pearl, Mississippi. The student killed two and wounded seven before Myrick could stop him. Why did it take Myrick so long to disarm the shooter? His gun was in his automobile, which was parked more than 1,000 feet from the school in compliance with the law.

The most heavily armed populations are the Swiss and the Israelis. Crime is negligible in both countries.

In January 2002, a disgruntled student at the Appalachian School of Law in Grundy, Virginia, shot and killed the dean, a professor, and a fellow student. He was disarmed and subdued before he could harm anyone else by two students who retrieved guns from their automobiles.

Utah and Oregon allow concealed-permit holders to carry their weapons on campus. To date, no school shooting incidents have occurred in these states.

The most heavily armed populations are the Swiss and the Israelis. Crime is negligible in both countries.

Frustration, pain, and other emotions shouldn't drive legislation; reason should.

The Luby's Cafeteria shootings in Killeen, Texas, on October 16, 1991, where a gunman killed 23 people, provide a stark example of the danger of gun-control laws. Suzanna Gratia Hupp, who was having lunch with her parents, left her gun in her car in compliance with state law. Her parents were among those killed. Two other diners also left their guns in their cars for fear of violating state law. Hupp had a clear shot at the killer several times as he reloaded and leisurely executed patrons.

"I was mad as hell at my legislators," she said, "because they had legislated me out of the right to protect myself and my family." Hupp is responsible for Texas's having enacted a concealed-carry law in 1995.

Be Prepared

How many more victims must be sacrificed on the altar of gun control? How many more Virginia Tech incidents must occur before common sense prevails? Blaming inanimate objects for criminal acts and legislating barriers to self-defense is foolish and self-destructive. The hostile atmosphere to gun possession and training fostered by gun-control advocates is costing lives. Frustration, pain, and other emotions shouldn't drive legislation; reason should. Though we may not be able to prevent such incidents, we can limit the damage they do.

Instead of listening to gun-control advocates whose advice brings death and injury, we would do better to abide by the Boy Scout motto: Be prepared!

11

Gun Control Does Not Influence Criminal Behavior or Reduce Crime Rates

John C. Moorhouse and Brent Wanner

John C. Moorhouse was a professor at Wake Forest University until 2007. Brent Wanner graduated from Wake Forest in May 2003 and Duke University in May 2009.

Gun control laws are complex, inconsistent, and have no impact on crime. State data reveals a lack of consistent enforcement at the state and local levels. Paradoxically an increase in crime leads to an increase in gun control regulations. The reasons gun control is not effective include the lack of influence that regulations have on criminal behavior. And there is no effective means to regulate the transfer of guns between non-dealer private parties.

Advocates argue that gun control laws reduce the incidence of violent crimes by reducing the prevalence of firearms. Gun laws control the types of firearms that may be purchased, designate the qualifications of those who may purchase and own a firearm, and restrict the safe storage and use of firearms. On this view, fewer guns mean less crime. Thus, there is a two-step linkage between gun control and crime rates: (1) the impact of gun control on the availability and accessibility of firearms, particularly handguns, and (2) the effect of the

John C. Moorhouse and Brent Wanner, "Does Gun Control Reduce Crime Or Does Crime Increase Gun Control?" *Cato Journal*, vol. 26, no. 1, Winter 2006, pp. 103–105, 121–122. Copyright © 2006 by Cato Institute. All rights reserved. Republished with permission of Cato Institute, conveyed through Copyright Clearance Center, Inc.

prevalence [availability] of guns on the commission of crimes. The direction of the effect runs from gun control to crime rates.

Conversely, because high crime rates are often cited as justifying more stringent gun control laws, high rates may generate political support for gun regulations. This suggests a causal effect running from crime rates to more stringent gun laws. But because ... relationships between gun control and crime rates unfold over time, they are not simultaneously determined in the usual econometric [statistical] sense. For example, crime rates in the early 1990s could be expected, ceteris paribus [all other things being equal] ... to influence the stringency of gun control measures in the late 1990s. In turn, more stringent gun control in the late 1990s could be expected, ceteris paribus, to affect crime rates several years later. Using state-level data, this article provides estimates of these twin relationships between gun control and crime rates.

Another reason for focusing on states is that 40 states prohibit or restrict local governments from enacting gun control ordinances.

Measuring the Degree of Gun Control

Researchers attempting to estimate the effect of gun control on crime rates face two problems. First, how is gun control to be measured? What is the empirical [testable] counterpart to gun control? Gun control is an umbrella term covering everything from laws prohibiting the ownership of defined classes of firearms to [laws] mandating the inclusion of gun locks with every firearm sold. These measures represent discrete legislative acts passed on different dates by different governing bodies. How do they interact to control the availability of firearms? Are the various measures complements or substitutes?

Second, the effectiveness of a particular gun control statute depends not only on its being on the books but the degree to which the law is enforced. Two jurisdictions may have the same gun control statute but experience very different effects, because in one of the jurisdictions little effort is devoted to enforcing the regulation. Enforcement of gun laws must be taken into account in order to accurately assess gun control.

State Laws Are Important

One contribution of this study is that it addresses these problems by using a comprehensive index of gun control laws for the 50 states and the District of Columbia. The index includes those laws in place in 1998. Normalized [standardized] to take on values of 0 to 100, the index is based on 30 weighted criteria applied to six categories of gun control regulations. The index was constructed as a project of the Open Society Institute's Center on Crime, Communities and Culture. The index "concentrates on states because most gun laws are state laws, though federal law also plays an important role." . . . Another reason for focusing on states is that 40 states prohibit or restrict local governments from enacting gun control ordinances.

Although there are literally thousands of state and local gun control statutes, the authors of the index group specific gun control measures into the following six categories. (1) Registration of firearms including purchase permits and gun registration of handguns and long guns (rifles and shotguns). (2) Safety training required before purchase. (3) Regulation of firearm sales including background checks, minimum age requirements for purchasing a firearm, a waiting period before a sale can be completed, one-gun-a-month limitation on purchases, all applied to long guns and/or handguns, plus a ban on "Saturday night specials," junk guns, and assault weapons. (4) Safe storage laws including child access prevention law. (5) Owner licensing for possession of handguns and/or long guns and minimum age restrictions for gun possession. (6) The presence of more restrictive municipal and county ordinances.

In addition, the index takes into account whether or not a law is effectively enforced. For example, while 32 states require background checks going beyond federal requirements, a number have no mechanism for ensuring that checks are made. Thus, the index distinguishes among states with no law, those with unenforced provisions, and those where the law is enforced. Furthermore, "In general, more points were assigned to 'upstream' measures [e.g., gun registration] than to 'downstream' measures [e.g., safe storage laws], to restrictions on handguns than to long guns, and to measures that facilitate the enforcement of the laws." . . .

Finally, if one wishes to study the effects of state gun control laws, using a carefully constructed index of gun control laws has several advantages. First, the effectiveness of a state's gun control laws may not be independent of the gun control regime [regulations] of neighboring states. If the citizens of state A can readily purchase guns in state B, then a spill-in [flowing over] effect may exist. Using an index provides a straightforward way of controlling for an adjacent state's gun control regime and estimating any spill-in effect. . . .

The fact remains that no careful empirical study, regardless of the type of data used, has found a negative relationship between gun control measures and crime rates.

Gun Control Is Ineffective

The empirical analysis presented here provides no support for the contention that gun control reduces crime rates. In none of the regressions [values] for the 10 categories of crime rates in 1999 and the 10 for 2001 is the measure of gun control statistically significant. The article tests another hypothesis, namely, that lax gun control laws in neighboring states undermine the effectiveness of state gun laws. It finds no support for this hypothesis. The proxy [substitute] for neighboring state gun control is never significant in any of the 20 regressions estimated.

By contrast, the article provides empirical support for the idea that high crime rates generate political support for the adoption [of] more stringent [rigid] gun controls. Moreover, there is empirical evidence that the probability of adopting more gun regulations is positively related to the proportion of Democrats in the state legislature.

The findings of this study that gun control is ineffective in reducing crime rates are consistent with the vast majority of other studies that use state data. . . . Moreover, state data do not mask the relationship flowing from high crime rates to the subsequent adoption of gun laws. The fact remains that no careful empirical study, regardless of the type of data used, has found a negative relationship between gun control measures and crime rates.

Assuming that gun control is ineffective, the question remains—why? The answer may be twofold. One, it might be that gun control simply does not influence the behavior of criminals in their efforts to obtain and use firearms. Law abiding citizens can be expected to conform to the law and obtain permits, register guns, and enroll in firearm safety courses. By contrast, there would be no surprise if it were found that criminals regularly violate the law by purchasing guns on illegal black markets or by stealing them.

Two, contemporary gun control measures typically attempt to influence the process of purchasing firearms at the point of sale between licensed dealers and their customers. Federal background checks, and often state background checks, waiting periods, and registration, are part of the process. But guns are long-lived capital assets. The stock of privately owned firearms in the United States is large relative to annual sales. Firearms are passed down through generations of family members. They are bought and sold, traded, parted out, and given away among friends, acquaintances, and strangers. It would be difficult, if not impossible, to constrain and regulate the transfer of firearms between non-dealer private parties. Gun control, while politically attractive because it appears to "deal directly with the problem," may in fact be a blunt instrument for reducing crime. Effective gun control may entail significant unintended consequences. Government extensive and intrusive enough to regulate all private transfers of firearms would raise significant civil liberties issues.

12

Public Acts of Gun Violence Do Not Change Opinions on Gun Control

Pew Research Center for the People & the Press

The Pew Research Center for the People & the Press is an independent opinion research group that studies attitudes toward the press, politics, and public policy issues. It is sponsored by the Pew Charitable Trusts and is one of seven projects that make up the Pew Research Center, a nonpartisan "fact tank" that provides information on the issues, attitudes, and trends shaping America and the world.

Public opinion about gun control is not affected by large-scale acts of violence. A majority of Americans oppose a ban on the sales of handguns. Mass shootings are seen by some Americans as a reflection of societal problems, while others view these tragedies as isolated acts of troubled individuals.

Last week's [April 16, 2007] shootings at Virginia Tech have had little immediate impact on public opinion about gun control. Six-in-ten Americans say it is more important to control gun ownership, while 32% say it is more important to protect the right of Americans to own guns. Opinion has changed little since 2004, when 58% said it was more important to control gun ownership than to protect the rights of gun owners.

Pew Research Center for the People & the Press, "News Release, April 23, 2007: VA Tech Shootings, Little Boost for Gun Control or Agreement on Causes," Washington, D.C.: Pew Research Center for the People & the Press, a project of the Pew Research Center, 2007. Copyright © 2007 Pew Research Center. Reproduced by permission.

At the same time, a 55% majority opposes a ban on the sale of handguns, while just 37% favor such a ban. There was greater support for gun control in the late 1990s and in 2000. In 2000, the public was evenly split over a handgun ban (47% favor/47% opposed).

The latest national survey by the Pew Research Center for the People & the Press, conducted April 18–22 [2007] among 1,508 adults, finds deep public differences about whether mass shootings like those at Virginia Tech reflect broader problems in society or are just the isolated acts of individuals.

Roughly half (47%) say such shootings are isolated acts, while about as many (46%) say they reflect broader societal problems. Opinions on this issue are divided politically; a solid majority of conservative Republicans (57%) say shootings like the one at Blacksburg [Virginia] are just the isolated acts of troubled individuals. Most liberal Democrats (59%) blame broader problems in American society.

Those who say the shootings reflect fundamental societal problems offer a variety of explanations. Overall, 37% volunteer problems related to morality or social values, while 23% cite shortcomings in the mental health, legal, or school systems. Just 14% mention gun laws or issues related to gun control.

People who said that the shootings at Virginia Tech and similar tragedies reflect broader problems in society differ in their views about those problems.

Gender Divide Over Causes

There is a sizable gender gap in opinions about whether the Virginia Tech shootings, and others like them, are isolated acts of troubled individuals or represent broader societal problems. By 55%–39%, men generally believe that such shootings are just isolated acts. By a nearly identical margin (54%–

37%), women say shootings like the one at Blacksburg reflect broader problems in American society.

While liberal Democrats generally say these tragedies reflect problems in society—and conservative Republicans say the opposite—other political groups are more evenly divided. Among independents, moderate and liberal Republicans, and conservative and moderate Democrats, roughly the same number points to broader societal problems as say these shootings are the isolated acts of troubled individuals.

Majorities have consistently said it is more important to control gun ownership than to protect the rights of gun owners, although opinions have fluctuated somewhat.

Notably, residents of the West are more likely than those in other regions to say that large-scale shootings are the acts of troubled people. People in the Northeast, by contrast, mostly point to broader societal problems.

People who said that the shootings at Virginia Tech and similar tragedies reflect broader problems in society differ in their views about those problems. Nearly half of Republicans who say the shootings reflect broader societal problems cite issues with morality or social values; that compares with just 26% of Democrats. Democrats who say the shootings reflect broader societal problems are much more likely than Republicans to mention gun laws or the ease with which people can buy guns (22% vs. 8%).

Gun Control Trends

In recent years, majorities have consistently said it is more important to control gun ownership than to protect the rights of gun owners, although opinions have fluctuated somewhat. Support for controlling gun ownership peaked in March 2000, less than a year after the shootings at Columbine High School. At that time, 66% said it was more important to control gun ownership, while just 29% thought it was more important to protect the rights of gun owners.

Support for gun owners' rights subsequently increased, reaching a high point of 42% in June 2003 before falling back to 37% in February 2004. Currently, there is somewhat less support for gun owners' rights than three years ago, though the overall balance of opinion has not changed substantially.

Yet there is somewhat greater opposition to a law banning the sale of handguns than there was in 2000 or the late 1990s. Currently, 55% say they oppose such a ban, compared with 47% in 2000. There are deep differences in opinions on both gun control questions. For instance, men oppose a ban on handgun sales by more than two-to-one (64%–30%). Women are fairly evenly divided over such a ban, with 47% opposed and 44% in favor.

By a wide margin (75%–21%), Republicans oppose a law banning handgun sales. Half of Democrats support a law prohibiting handgun sales, while 43% are opposed. Most independents (54%) oppose a ban on handgun sales, while 38% support a ban.

Impact on Children

Most parents of school age children say their kids have followed coverage of the shootings (56%), and most have talked either a lot (19%) or some (39%) with their children about the events at Virginia Tech. At the same time, four-in-ten parents of children in Kindergarten through 12th grade say their kids have not followed the story, and 24% say they have not talked about the events with their kids at all.

Four-in-ten parents say they have been trying to restrict how much coverage of the shootings their children watch, while 58% have not. Mothers are significantly more likely to say they are trying to restrict how much their kids see than are fathers (46% vs. 32%).

Most parents with children in college also report talking either a lot (27%) or some (28%) about the Virginia Tech shootings with their children, but about a quarter (28%) have not talked about the incident with their college kids at all. Most college parents (57%) say their kids in college have expressed no fears about safety at their school since the shootings, while 10% say their children in college have expressed a lot of concern about safety.

13

State & Local Governments Must Overcome Federal Gun Law Deficiencies

Legal Community Against Violence

Legal Community Against Violence is a national public interest law center dedicated to preventing gun violence and serving activists and public officials to achieve policy reform at the state and local levels.

In its ruling in District of Columbia v. Heller, *the U.S. Supreme Court "held that the Second Amendment confers an individual right to possess firearms unrelated to service in a well-regulated state militia." This is an about-face from the "Court's [1939] interpretation of the Second Amendment in* United States v. Miller." *The Second Amendment interpreted as it is in* Heller *does not confer an unlimited right and applies only to the federal government. In light of* Heller, *it is important to promote at the state and local levels of government "effective, common sense laws as a means to reduce the growing gun violence epidemic in our country."* The views expressed in "Gun Regulation and the Second Amendment—Moving Forward After *District of Columbia v. Heller*," excerpted below, are those of Legal Community Against Violence. The publication is not intended as legal advice to any person or entity, and should not be regarded as such.

The *District of Columbia v. Heller* Decision

In 2003, Dick Anthony Heller and other plaintiffs challenged the District of Columbia's decades-old laws banning possession of handguns and requiring firearms in the home to be stored locked or disassembled. After the D.C. Circuit Court of Appeals ruled the laws unconstitutional under the Second Amendment[1]—the only time a federal appellate court had ever invalidated a gun law on Second Amendment grounds— the U.S. Supreme Court agreed to hear the case. This set the stage for the Court's first ruling on the Second Amendment in almost 70 years.

The Court's Holding

The Supreme Court issued its historic decision in *District of Columbia v. Heller* on June 26, 2008.[2] In a 5–4 ruling written by Justice Antonin Scalia, the Court held that the Second Amendment confers an individual right to possess firearms unrelated to service in a well-regulated state militia. The Court struck down the District's ban on handgun possession, finding that "the inherent right of self-defense has been central to the Second Amendment" and that handguns are "overwhelmingly chosen by American society" for self-defense in the home, "where the need for defense of self, family, and property is most acute."[3] The Court also struck down the District's requirement that firearms in the home be stored unloaded and disassembled or bound by a trigger lock or similar device, because the law contained no exception for self-defense.

An Abrupt About-Face from Prior Precedent

The Court's ruling in *District of Columbia v. Heller* represents a radical departure from the Court's previous interpretation of the Second Amendment in *United States v. Miller*, 307 U.S. 174 (1939). In the *Miller* case, the Court stated, in a unanimous decision, that the "obvious purpose" of the Second

Amendment was to "assure the continuation and render possible the effectiveness of" the state militia, and the Amendment "must be interpreted and applied with that end in view."[4] In reliance on *Miller*, hundreds of lower federal and state appellate courts have rejected Second Amendment challenges to our nation's gun laws over the last seven decades.[5]

"A well regulated Militia, being necessary to the security of a free State, the right of the people to keep and bear Arms, shall not be infringed." — Second Amendment to the U.S. Constitution

---

The Right Is Not Unlimited

Although the *Heller* decision establishes a new individual right to "keep and bear arms," the opinion makes clear that the right is not unlimited, and should not be understood as "a right to keep and carry any weapon whatsoever in any manner whatsoever and for whatever purpose."[6] The Court provides examples of gun laws that it deems "presumptively lawful" under the Second Amendment, including those which:

- Prohibit the possession of firearms by felons and the mentally ill;

- Forbid firearm possession in sensitive places such as schools and government buildings;

- Impose conditions on the commercial sale of firearms.

The Court makes clear that this list is not exhaustive.[7] The Court also concludes that the Second Amendment is consistent with laws banning "dangerous and unusual weapons" not "in common use at the time," such as M-16 rifles and other firearms that are most useful in military service.[8] Finally, the Court declares that its analysis should not be read to suggest "the invalidity of laws regulating the storage of firearms to prevent accidents."[9]

The Standard of Review

The *Heller* decision fails to articulate a legal standard of review, or test, to be applied in evaluating other laws under the Second Amendment. Thus, the decision provides little guidance to lower courts or legislators, creating new uncertainty in this area and inviting litigation.[10]

The Second Amendment Applies Only to the Federal Government

Because *Heller* considered laws of the District of Columbia (a federal enclave), the Court stated that the question of whether the Second Amendment applies to the states is "a question not presented by this case."[11] While the *Heller* Court did not rule on whether the Second Amendment applies to state or local governments, the Court did note its earlier decisions holding that "the Second Amendment applies only to the Federal Government."[12] These decisions remain the law of the land.

> *Following the* Heller *decision, we must redouble our efforts at the state and local levels to promote effective, commonsense laws as a means to reduce the growing gun violence epidemic in our country.*

What the Decision Means for Our Nation's Gun Laws

While the *Heller* decision leaves many questions unanswered, one thing is clear: Gun regulation is alive and well in the United States. Elected officials and community leaders can feel confident that most common sense gun laws will be upheld. A strong legislative record—including facts regarding the problem sought to be addressed and the reasons why the proposed law is an appropriate response—is critical to maximizing the likelihood that a gun law be affirmed by the courts. Given our nation's tragic epidemic of gun violence, elected officials should have no difficulty describing the problem. The undisputed facts show:

- More than 30,000 Americans die from firearm-related injuries each year—an average of 80 deaths each day.[13]—and nearly 70,000 others are treated for gunshot wounds.[14]

- Young people up to 24 years of age constitute over 40% of all firearm deaths and non-fatal injuries each year.[15] The number of children and teens in America killed by guns in 2005 would fill 120 public school classrooms of 25 students each.[16]

- On average, 46 gun suicides were committed each day for the years 1999-2005. During that time, over 5,300 people in the United States died from unintentional shootings.[17]

- The U.S. has the highest rate of firearm deaths among 25 high-income nations.[18]

- Guns are used to commit nearly 400,000 crimes every year and nearly 70% of all murders in the U.S. are committed with a firearm.[19]

- Medical costs related to gun violence are estimated at $2.3 billion annually, half of which are borne by American taxpayers.[20] Factoring in all the direct and indirect medical, legal and societal costs, the annual cost of gun violence in our nation amounts to $100 billion.[21]

Fortunately, a variety of common sense regulatory options exist to address this national crisis. Many jurisdictions across the country already have adopted laws to require background checks on all gun purchasers; to ensure that guns are not sold to criminals and other prohibited purchasers; to prohibit the sale of military-style weapons (such as assault weapons and 50 caliber rifles); to require gun owners to obtain a license and register their firearms; to regulate guns as a consumer product; and to regulate firearms dealers through licensing and other requirements.

Legal Community Against Violence (LCAV) believes that these types of laws and many others should be upheld as consistent with the Supreme Court's holding in the *Heller* case.

Notes

  [1] *Parker v. District of Columbia*, 478 F.3d 370 (D.C. Cir. 2007).

  [2] *District of Columbia v. Heller*, 128 S. Ct. 2783 (2008).

  [3] *Id.* at 2817.

  [4] *United States v. Miller*, 307 U.S. 174, 178 (1939).

  [5] The *Heller* Court dismissed the *Miller* case as not "a thorough examination" of the Second Amendment, and limited *Miller* to the proposition that "the Second Amendment does not protect those weapons not typically possessed by law-abiding citizens for lawful purposes, such as short-barreled shotguns." *Heller, supra* note 2, at 2814.

  [6] *Id.* at 2816.

  [7] *Id.* at 2817 n. 26.

  [8] *Id.* at 2817.

  [9] *Id.* at 2820.

  [10] Immediately after the *Heller* decision was issued, the gun lobby filed suits challenging handgun possession bans in San Francisco, Chicago and other Illinois communities. The San Francisco prohibition applies only to public housing.

  [11] *Heller, supra* note 2, at 2813 n. 23.

  [12] *Id.,* citing *Miller v. Texas*, 153 U.S. 535, 538 (1894); *Presser v. Illinois*, 116 U.S. 252, 265 (1886); and *United States v. Cruikshank*, 92 U.S. 542 (1876).

[13] U.S. Department of Health and Human Services, Centers for Disease Control and Prevention, National Center for Injury Prevention and Control, Web-Based Injury Statistics Query & Reporting System *(WISQARS), WISQARS Injury Mortality Reports, 1999–2005 (2008)*, at http://webappa.cdc.gov/sasweb/ncipc/mortrate10_sy.html.

[14] U.S. Department of Health and Human Services, Centers for Disease Control and Prevention, National Center for Injury Prevention and Control, Web-Based Injury Statistics Query & Reporting System (*WISQARS*), *WISQARS Nonfatal Injury Reports (2008)*, at http://webappa.cdc.gov/sasweb/ncipc/nfirates2001.html.

[15] *Id.*; *WISQARS Injury Mortality Reports, 1999–2005, supra* note 13.

[16] *Id.*

[17] *Id.*

[18] Wendy Cukier and Victor W. Sidel, *The Global Gun Epidemic: From Saturday Night Specials to AK-47s*, 17 (2006).

[19] U.S. Department of Justice, Bureau of Justice Statistics, *Key Facts at a Glance: Crimes Committed with Firearms, 1973–2006*, at http://www.ojp.usdoj.gov/bjs/glance/tables/guncrimetab.htm.

[20] Philip J. Cook et al., *The Medical Costs of Gunshot Injuries in the United States*, 282 JAMA 447 (Aug. 4, 1999).

[21] Philip Cook and Jens Ludwig, *Gun Violence: The Real Costs* 115 (2000).

14

Gun Ownership Should Be Privately Regulated

Peter A. Gudmundsson

Peter A. Gudmundsson, a hunter and gun owner, is chief executive officer of Beckett Media in Dallas, Texas.

The opposing positions in the gun control debate tend to take all or nothing stances; and with no room for compromise, little progress can be made in the way of gun safety. A private certification practice—which has been productive for scuba divers—that includes training and background checks before an individual can own a gun, may be the answer to safety and a successful firearms industry.

The Supreme Court will issue a major interpretation of the Second Amendment in coming weeks. But even as both sides in the gun debate await the *D.C. v. Heller* ruling, the gun industry should set its sights on a different target: certification. [Editor's note: In June 2008 the Court sustained the right to possess a firearm and to use it lawfully.]

It should develop and adopt a private licensing and certification program fashioned on the highly successful scuba diving industry model to provide safety, legal, and marksmanship training to all gun owners and users. Such a private mandate will ensure a base of safer and more knowledgeable gun users and develop a fresh and lucrative revenue source for the whole industry.

Peter A. Gudmundsson, "What the Gun Industry Can Learn from Scuba Divers," *Christian Science Monitor*, April 29, 2008. Reproduced by permission of the author.

The Debate's Extremes Have Prevented Progress

For decades, the debate on gun control in America has been defined by polar opposite political positions. On the left, gun ownership abolitionists seek the intervention of government to severely restrict or outlaw firearms possession and use. With strong support among coastal urban populations and high-income elites, these gun-control advocates appeal to the inherent evil of gun violence as proof of the desirability of severely restricting access to guns. Their argument is moralistic and practical, if altogether naive given the millions of firearms already present in American homes—and the ease of obtaining guns for criminal purposes.

All retailers of guns and/or ammunition would require the provision of such private certification by the consumer before consenting to the sale of any of those items.

On the other side, defiant gun owners and libertarians cite constitutional justification—and anachronistic biblical and patriotic frontier mythological imagery—to bolster their possession of an immutable right to "keep and bear arms." With such a political impasse of instinctive and deep mistrust, there is no wonder that little progress [has] been made in making our homes, streets, and fields safer from the real dangers of legal and illegal firearms use. The core of this problem derives from the absolutist nature of both camps. It is simply "No restrictions" versus "complete regulation or abolition."

Enter the scuba model. For decades, the international scuba diving community has required all divers to obtain certifications from one of two private associations, the National Association of Underwater Instructors [or] the Professional Association of Diving Instructors. No diver may fill their tanks or take part in recreational or professional diving trips without first obtaining a certification card from one of these private organizations. For their part, dive shops and schools generate significant portions of their revenue from the tuition that would-be divers pay to obtain their certifications at basic to advanced levels. Undergoing classroom instruction, pool lessons, and "open water" testing, graduates of these programs are thoroughly trained in all aspects of safety and proper procedure in what would otherwise be an inherently dangerous pastime.

Firearms Certification Would Be Private, but Comprehensive

The gun industry, perhaps led by the National Rifle Association, should develop a curriculum of training and education leading to firearms certification. All retailers of guns and/or ammunition would require the provision of such private certification by the consumer before consenting to the sale of any of those items. Background checks should be included in the certification process as well as periodic refresher courses. The federal and state governments would not be involved. Records of gun ownership would be available to government or law-enforcement officials only with the written consent of the certified owner or a warrant provided by proper authority. Non-consenting retailers would be "blackballed" by industry leaders and cut off from supplies of goods and services.

The firearms industry has an unprecedented opportunity to show leadership and creativity at this time when the debate is otherwise deadlocked. More safety and additional revenue for gun ranges and stores makes for a healthier industry that will have better success at attracting new sportsmen and customers.

15

Both Sides of the Gun Debate Would Benefit from Compromise

Rachel Graves

Rachel Graves has been involved in political and investigative reporting, and she is writing a book called The Gun Follies.

In the gun control debate, the opposing sides fuel each other's fight, mutually empowering polarized arguments. But in the country's best interests, a middle ground exists that could maintain safe gun use and prevent unnecessary gun violence. The debaters should leave behind the unproductive cycle and make a working compromise.

Two years ago, Florida enacted a law that allows anyone who feels threatened anywhere to use deadly force. Today the National Rifle Association (NRA) is shepherding similar laws through legislatures across the country.

The so-called Castle Doctrine extended the notion of a man's home being his castle to public streets being his castle. When the law first went into effect in October 2005, the nation's most prominent gun-control group, the Brady Campaign, decided to fight back. Sort of.

An Unequal Struggle over Gun Control

The Brady Campaign—understaffed, underfunded, and generally floundering—missed the news of the law's consideration until it was almost a done deal. In behavior typical for both

Rachel Graves, "Gun Debate Muzzles the Middle Ground," *Christian Science Monitor*, September 5, 2007. Reproduced by permission of the author.

sides in a war of words, the gun-control group's inability to keep the legislation from passing did not stop the group from using the occasion to ratchet up the rhetoric.

The Brady Campaign put up a billboard in Miami that October, took out ads in cold climates where people often take Florida vacations, and handed out fliers at Florida airports— all warning tourists of their possible demise on their trips to Florida beaches and Disney World.

The dirty secret of both sides in the gun debate is that, without a powerful enemy, they cannot woo supporters or raise money.

The campaign got the biggest reaction in Britain and Canada, where it fit perfectly into the notion of Americans as barbarians. A headline in the British *Birmingham Post* read, "Going to Florida? Beware the gun-happy locals."

Although Florida officials were unhappy about a potential blow to tourism, the bigger upset was that the Brady Campaign's move played right into the NRA's hands.

The dirty secret of both sides in the gun debate is that, without a powerful enemy, they cannot woo supporters or raise money. They are like boxers in a ring—propping each other up even as they try to get in blows. They are locked in an antagonistic embrace that creates gridlock on solving the nation's gun problems.

Of course, it is not an embrace of equals. The NRA has a $200 million annual budget, while the Brady Campaign's is $8 million. Since 1990, according to the Center for Responsive Politics, gun rights groups have given $18.7 billion to political candidates, while gun control groups have given only $1.7 billion.

In fact, no one knows whether shootings have increased in Florida as a result of the Castle Doctrine because the Brady Campaign and other interested groups cannot afford to have lawyers track the results. Paradoxically, the NRA's Goliath status forces the group to work harder to make people believe that it has potent enemies—a challenge to which it has risen. The cover of one issue of *America's 1st Freedom*, one of the NRA's several magazines, threatened that the United Nations will seize Americans' guns, an idea that is laughably implausible. The NRA also exaggerates the impact of other stock enemies, including the Brady Campaign itself, the French, and New York Mayor Michael Bloomberg, who is trying single-handedly to curb the flow of illegal guns into his city.

After Hurricane Katrina, officials tried to ban guns from the streets of New Orleans and from temporary housing for refugees. The NRA halted the efforts in federal court. Wayne LaPierre, the NRA's chief executive officer, painted the attempts to check violence as proof that the US government would take away its citizens' guns.

"To stop such civil disarmaments—the greatest threat of all—will require massive NRA member pressure at every level of government," Mr. LaPierre wrote in his monthly letter to NRA members. "In these upcoming battles, our battle cry must be *Remember New Orleans!* Never, ever forget."

Reasonable people can oppose civilian ownership of machine guns or .50-caliber rifles ... while still supporting hunting and owning guns for self-defense.

The Middle Ground Has Been Ignored

Certainly, most Americans would say that the shootings at Virginia Tech [in which a student gunman killed 32 people] should never, ever be forgotten either. But somehow, though school shootings continue, though an average of 32 homicides are committed with guns in the United States each day, though dozens of suspected terrorists are known to have passed background checks to legally purchase guns, the gun-control side cannot gain traction.

Instead the bluster and bickering continue. The warring lobbying groups call each other "gun grabbers," "enemies of freedom," and "gun zealots."

"The two sides in this debate behave like spoiled children who won't sit at the table together and play nice," admits Peter Hamm, the spokesman for the Brady Campaign.

What the two sides don't acknowledge is that reasonable people can oppose civilian ownership of machine guns or .50-caliber rifles so powerful they must be shot using a tripod while still supporting hunting and owning guns for self-defense. Americans can support background checks on guns sold everywhere—not just by licensed dealers—without putting gun companies out of business. The United States can require registration of guns and proficiency tests for gun owners, just as we do with cars, without making it impossible, or even difficult, for law-abiding citizens to buy guns.

The name-calling and breath-holding have made us all forget that a middle ground is possible.

Organizations to Contact

The editors have compiled the following list of organizations concerned with the issues debated in this book. The descriptions are derived from materials provided by the organizations. All have publications or information available for interested readers. The list was compiled on the date of publication of the present volume; the information provided here may change. Be aware that many organizations take several weeks or longer to respond to inquiries, so allow as much time as possible.

American Civil Liberties Union (ACLU)
125 Broad Street, 18th Floor, New York, NY   10004-2400
(212) 549-2500
e-mail: aclu@aclu.org
Web site: www.aclu.org

The ACLU champions the rights set forth in the U.S. Constitution and the Bill of Rights. The union interprets the Second Amendment as a guarantee to form militias, not as a guarantee of the individual right to own and bear firearms, and believes that gun control is constitutional and necessary. The ACLU publishes the semiannual *Civil Liberties* in addition to policy statements and reports, many of which are available on its Web site.

Brady Campaign to Prevent Gun Violence and Brady Center to Prevent Gun Violence
1225 I Street NW, Suite 1100, Washington, DC   20005
Campaign: (202) 898-0792; Center: (202) 289-7319 • Campaign fax: (202) 371-9615; Center fax: (202) 408-1851
Web sites: www.bradycampaign.org; www.bradycenter.com

The primary goal of both the Brady Campaign and the Brady Center is to create an America free from gun violence. Through grassroots activism both organizations work to reform the gun industry, educate the public about gun violence, and develop sensible regulations to reduce gun violence. The organizations publish fact sheets, issue briefs, and special reports on their Web sites, including "No Check. No Gun" and "Domestic Violence and Guns."

Cato Institute
1000 Massachusetts Ave. NW, Washington, DC 20001
(202) 842-0200 • fax: (202) 842-3490
e-mail: librarian@cato.org
Web site: www.cato.org

The Cato Institute is a libertarian public-policy research foundation. It evaluates government policies and offers reform proposals and commentary on its Web site. Its publications include such articles as "Fighting Back: Crime, Self-Defense, and the Right to Carry a Handgun" and "Trust the People: The Case Against Gun Control." It also publishes the magazine *Regulation,* the *Cato Policy Report,* and such books as *The Samurai, the Mountie, and the Cowboy: Should America Adopt the Gun Controls of Other Democracies?*

Citizens Committee for the Right to Keep and Bear Arms
12500 NE Tenth Place, Bellevue, WA 98005
(425) 454-4911 • fax: (425) 451-3959
e-mail: InformationRequest@ccrkba.org
Web site: www.ccrkba.org

The committee believes that the U.S. Constitution's Second Amendment guarantees and protects the right of individual Americans to own guns. It works to educate the public concerning this right and to lobby legislators to prevent the passage of gun-control laws. The committee is affiliated with the Second Amendment Foundation and has more than six hundred thousand members. It publishes several magazines, including *Gun Week, Women & Guns,* and *Gun News Digest.* News releases, fact sheets, editorial columns from *Women & Guns,* and "Hindsight" editorials from *Gun Week* are available on its Web site.

Coalition for Gun Control

PO Box 90062, Toronto, Ontario   M6K 3K3
  Canada
(416) 604-0209 (Toronto); (514) 725-2021 (Montreal)
e-mail: 71417.763@compuserve.com (Toronto); cgc.montreal@
compuserve.com (Montreal)
Web site: www.guncontrol.ca

This Canadian organization formed to reduce gun death, injury, and crime. It supports strict safe-storage requirements, possession permits, a complete ban on assault weapons, and tougher restrictions on handguns. The coalition publishes press releases and backgrounders. Its Web site provides information on firearms death and injury, illegal gun trafficking, and Canada's gun-control law.

Coalition to Stop Gun Violence (CSGV)

1424 L Street NW, Suite 2-1, Washington, DC   20005
(202) 408-0061
Web site: www.csgv.org

CSGV lobbies at the local, state, and federal levels to ban the sale of handguns to individuals and to institute licensing and registration of all firearms. It also litigates cases against firearms makers. Its publications include various informational sheets on gun violence and the *Annual Citizens' Conference to Stop Gun Violence Briefing Book*, a compendium of gun-control fact sheets, arguments, and resources. On its Web site, CSGV publishes articles on assault weapons, gun laws, and other gun violence issues.

Gun Owners of America (GOA)

8001 Forbes Place, Suite 102, Springfield, VA   22151
(703) 321-8585 • fax: (703) 321-8408
e-mail: goamail@gunowners.org
Web site: http://gunowners.org

GOA is a nonprofit lobbying organization that defends the Second Amendment rights of gun owners. It has developed a network of attorneys to help fight court battles to protect gun owner rights. GOA also works with members of Congress, state legislators, and local citizens to protect gun ranges and local gun clubs from closure by the government. On its Web site the organization publishes fact sheets and links to op-ed articles, including "People Don't Stop Killers, People With Guns Do" and "Is Arming Teachers the Solution to School Shootings?"

Independence Institute
13952 Denver West Parkway, Suite 400, Golden, CO 80401
(303) 279-6536 • fax: (303) 279-4176
e-mail: kay@i2i.org
Web site: www.i2i.org

The institute is a pro-free market think tank that supports gun ownership as both a civil liberty and a constitutional right. Its Web site offers articles, fact sheets, and commentary from a variety of sources, including "Making Schools Safe for Criminals," "Is Gun Control a New Religion?" and "Kids and Guns: The Politics of Panic."

Jews for the Preservation of Firearms Ownership (JPFO)
PO Box 270143, Hartford, WI 53027
(262) 673-9745 • fax: (262) 673-9746
e-mail: jpfo@jpfo.org
Web site: www.jpfo.org

JPFO is an educational organization that believes Jewish law mandates self-defense. Its primary goal is the elimination of the idea that gun control is a socially useful public policy in any country. On its Web site JPFO provides links to firearms commentary.

National Crime Prevention Council (NCPC)
2345 Crystal Drive, Suite 500, Arlington, VA 22202-4801
(202) 466-6272
Web site: www.ncpc.org

The NCPC is a branch of the U.S. Department of Justice. Through its programs and educational materials, the council works to teach Americans how to reduce crime and to address its causes. It provides readers with information on gun control and gun violence. The NCPC's publications include the newsletter *Catalyst*, which is published ten times a year, plus articles, brochures, and fact sheets, many of which are available on its Web site.

National Rifle Association of America (NRA)
11250 Waples Mill Road, Fairfax, VA   22030
(703) 267-1000; 800-392-8683 • fax: (703) 267-3989
Web site: www.nra.org

With nearly three million members, the NRA is America's largest organization of gun owners. It is also the primary lobbying group for those who oppose gun-control laws. The NRA believes that such laws violate the U.S. Constitution and do nothing to reduce crime. In addition to its monthly magazines *America's 1st Freedom, American Rifleman, American Hunter, InSights*, and *Shooting Sports USA*, the NRA publishes numerous books, bibliographies, reports, and pamphlets on gun ownership, gun safety, and gun control, some of which are available on its Web site.

PAX / Real Solutions to Gun Violence
100 Wall Street, 2nd Floor, New York, NY   10005
(212) 269-5100; 1(800) 983-4275
e-mail: info@paxusa.org; ask@paxusa.org; speakup@paxusa.org
Web site: www.paxusa.org

PAX is a nonprofit organization working to help bring an end to gun violence against children and families. PAX launched the ASK campaign to encourage parents to determine if guns are in the homes where their children are visiting. The SPEAK UP campaign encourages students to report weapon-related threats in their schools and neighborhoods to the organization's national hotline.

Second Amendment Foundation
12500 NE Tenth Place, Bellevue, WA   98005
(425) 454-7012 • fax: (425) 451-3959

e-mail: adminforweb@saf.org
Web site: www.saf.org

A sister organization to the Citizens Committee for the Right to Keep and Bear Arms, the foundation is dedicated to informing Americans about their Second Amendment right to keep and bear firearms. It believes that gun-control laws violate this right. The foundation publishes numerous books, including *Armed: New Perspectives on Gun Control, CCW: Carrying Concealed Weapons*, and *The Concealed Handgun Manual: How To Choose, Carry, and Shoot a Gun in Self Defense*. Reports, articles, and commentary on gun issues are available on its Web site.

U.S. Department of Justice, Office of Justice Programs
810 Seventh Street NW, Washington, DC   20531
Phone and e-mail for specific bureaus and offices are available at www.ojp.usdoj.gov/home/contactus.htm;
Web site: www.ojp.usdoj.gov

The Department of Justice (DOJ) strives to protect citizens by maintaining effective law enforcement, crime prevention, crime detection, and prosecution and rehabilitation of offenders. Through its Office of Justice Programs, the department operates the National Institute of Justice, the Office of Juvenile Justice and Delinquency Prevention, and the Bureau of Justice Statistics. The Bureau of Justice Statistics provides research on crime and criminal justice. The offices of the DOJ publish a variety of crime-related documents on their respective Web sites.

Violence Policy Center
1730 Rhode Island Ave. NW, Suite 1014
Washington, DC   20036
(202) 822-8200
Web site: www.vpc.org

The center is an educational foundation that conducts research on firearms violence. It works to educate the public concerning the dangers of guns and supports gun-control measures. The center's publications include *Drive-By America, A Shrinking Minority: The Continuing Decline of Gun Ownership in America*, and *When Men Murder Women: An Analysis of 2005 Homicide Data*. On the center's Web site, it publishes fact sheets, press releases, and studies on concealed carry laws, assault weapons, and other firearm-violence issues.

Bibliography

Books

Joan Burbick   *Gun Show Nation: Gun Culture and American Democracy*. New York: New Press, 2006.

Donna Dees-Thomases and Alison Hendrie   *Looking for a Few Good Moms: How One Mother Rallied A Million Others Against the Gun Lobby*. Emmaus, PA: Rodale, 2004.

Brian Doherty   *Gun Control on Trial: Inside the Supreme Court Battle over the Second Amendment*. Washington, D.C.: Cato Institute, 2008.

Richard Feldman   *Ricochet: Confessions of a Gun Lobbyist*. Hoboken, NJ: Wiley, 2007.

Alan M. Gottlieb and Dave Workman   *These Dogs Don't Hunt: The Democrats' War On Guns*. Bellevue, WA: Merril Press, 2008.

Arnold Grossman   *One Nation Under Guns, an Essay on an American Epidemic*. Golden, CO: Fulcrum, 2006.

Stephen P. Halbrook   *The Founders' Second Amendment: Origins of the Right to Bear Arms*. Chicago, IL: Ivan R. Dee, 2008.

David Hemenway   *Private Guns, Public Health*. Ann Arbor, MI: University of Michigan Press, 2006.

Douglas Kellner   *Guys And Guns Amok: Domestic Terrorism and School Shootings from the Oklahoma City Bombing to the Virginia Tech Massacre.* Boulder, CO: Paradigm, 2008.

Caitlin Kelly   *Blown Away: American Women and Guns.* New York: Pocket, 2004.

Alan Korwin and   *The Heller Case: Gun Rights Affirmed.*
David B. Kopel   Phoenix, AZ: Bloomfield Press, 2008.

Richard Labunski   *James Madison and the Struggle for the Bill of Rights.* New York: Oxford University Press, 2008.

Kekla Magoon   *Gun Control.* Edina, MN: ABDO, 2007.

Jeffrey D. Monroe   *Homicide and Gun Control: The Brady Handgun Violence Prevention Act and Homicide Rates.* El Paso, TX: LFB Scholarly Publishing, 2008.

Lucinda Roy   *No Right to Remain Silent: The Tragedy at Virginia Tech.* New York: Harmony, 2009.

Mark V. Tushnet   *Out of Range: Why the Constitution Can't End the Battle over Guns.* New York: Oxford University Press, 2007.

Harry L. Wilson   *Guns, Gun Control, and Elections: The Politics and Policy of Firearms.* Lanham, MD: Rowman & Littlefield, 2006.

Periodicals

Joan Biskupic and Kevin Johnson	"Landmark Ruling Fires Challenges to Gun Laws," *USA Today*, June 27, 2008.
Geoff Brown	"Cities Under Fire," *Johns Hopkins Public Health*, Fall 2008.
Brad Cain	"Lawmakers Move to Close Gun Permit Records," *The World*, February 23, 2009.
Bob Egelko	"Ruling's Ricochet, A Right to Own Guns: Supreme Court Defines 2nd Amendment—Gun Lobby Expected to Challenge S.F. Ban on Handgun Possession in Public," *San Francisco Chronicle*, June 27, 2008.
Annette Fuentes	"Guns Don't Make Homes Safer," *The Progressive*, July 2, 2008.
Deborah Hastings	"Licensed to Kill? Gunmen in Killings Had Permits," *The Washington Post*, April 7, 2009.
Ashley Johnson	"Guns out of Control," *The Atlantic*, June 26, 2008.
Allison Kasic	"DC Gun Ban Lift Empowers Women," *Independent Women's Forum*, July 7, 2008.
Jim Kessler	"Deepen Gun Ownership," *Democracy, a Journal of Ideas*, Spring 2008.

Dave Kopel   "Conservative Activists Key to DC Handgun Decision," *Human Events*, June 27, 2008.

Wayne LaPierre   "Self-Defense Is a Basic Human Right," *National Rifle Association/Political Victory Fund*, April 3, 2008.

Daniel Lazare   "Arms and the Right," *The Nation*, April 17, 2008.

Michael A. Lindenberger   "Ten Years After Columbine, It's Easier to Bear Arms," *Time*, April 20, 2009.

Adam Liptak   "Gun Laws and Crime: A Complex Relationship," *The New York Times*, June 29, 2009.

Nelson Lund   "The Second Amendment Comes Before the Supreme Court: The Issues and the Arguments," *The Heritage Foundation*, March 14, 2008.

Warren Richey   "The Historic 5 to 4 Ruling Says the Right to Bear Arms Applies to Individuals," *The Christian Science Monitor*, June 27, 2008.

Amanda Ripley   "Ignoring Virginia Tech," *Time*, April 15, 2008.

Lydia Saad   "Before Recent Shootings, Gun-Control Support Was Fading," *Gallup, Inc.*, April 8, 2009.

Jake Smilovitz   "To Push Gun Rights, Group Offers a Gun Voucher," *The Michigan Daily*, November 12, 2007.

James Taranto   "How a Young Lawyer Saved the Second Amendment," *Wall Street Journal*, July 19, 2008.

Stuart Taylor, Jr.   "Recent Supreme Court Decisions Show," *Newsweek*, July 7–14, 2008.

Robert VerBruggen   "Repeal the Second Amendment?" *The American Spectator*, December 3, 2007.

Edwin Vieira, Jr.   "Gun Rights on Trial," *The New American*, September 1, 2008.

Nicholas Wapshott   "Disney Under Fire, Battle Lines Have Been Drawn After a Disney Employee Was Sacked for Bringing a .45-Calibre Pistol to Work," *New Statesman*, July 31, 2008.

Drew Westen   "Guns on the Brain," *The American Prospect*, July 13, 2007.

Index